AUTHOR SUCCESS HABITS

THE THREE ESSENTIAL HABITS OF HIGHLY SUCCESSFUL AUTHORS

SALLY MILLER

FREE BONUS

As a thank you for buying my book, I have created a bonus area to help you on your journey. The bonus area has a growing list of resources that will help you:

> Implement the habits you need to become a highly successful author

> Finally stop spinning your wheels and self-publish your first non-fiction book

> Establish a successful home business that won't suck up all your time

Download your bonus resources at sallyannmiller.com/publish

Copyright © 2020 by Sally Miller

All rights reserved.

No part of this publication may be reproduced, distributed, or transmitted in any form or by any means, including photocopying, recording, or other electronic or mechanical methods, without the prior written permission of the publisher, except in the case of brief quotations embodied in reviews and certain other non-commercial uses permitted by copyright law.

The information provided within this book is for general informational purposes only. While the authors try to keep the information up-to-date and correct, there are no representations or warranties, express or implied, about the completeness, accuracy, reliability, suitability or availability with respect to the information, products, services, or related graphics contained in this book for any purpose. Any use of this information is at your own risk.

Any advice that is provided in this book is based on the experience of the authors and does not reflect the opinion of the distributor. All opinions expressed in this book are solely the opinion of the authors.

Disclaimer

Some of the links in this book may be affiliate links. If you click them and decide to buy something, we may be paid a commission. This won't cost you any extra. We only include links to products or services

CONTENTS

1. Introduction	1
2. The Three Habits	6
Section One	11
3. Why You Write	12
4. Author Business Strategy	21
5. Set Extraordinary Goals	31
6. Achieve Your Goals	36
Section Two	44
7. Becoming Superhuman	45
8. Write Quickly and Easily	50
9. Your Publishing Process	58
10. Sell More Books	63
Section Three	72
11. Take Charge of Your Life	73
12. Watch Your Brain	81
13. Becoming Fearless	88
14. Positive Action	94
15. Conclusion	101
About the Author	103

1

INTRODUCTION

A child has no trouble believing the unbelievable, nor does the genius or the madman. It's only you and I, with our big brains and our tiny hearts, who doubt and overthink and hesitate.

— STEVEN PRESSFIELD

You're a writer. Perhaps you're already a published author, or you dream of becoming one. If this is you, then you're also familiar with fear. How do I know this? Because all creators who share their work experience self-doubt. Unless—as Pressfield informs us—you're a child, a genius, or a madman.

The moment you step into the arena, the internal chatter starts up. Your brain commands you to run and hide. It questions your every move. You feel exposed, as if you're standing naked in front of family, friends, and strangers. Your creation is on display for everyone to see.

This is when most people slam on the brakes. Maybe you withdraw into your cave. You decide not to publish, or you delay and spend more time perfecting your work. Eventually, you might power onward and publish your book. But you're cautious with your marketing efforts. You turn down the volume on your voice and your dreams.

This is the greatest disservice you can do the world. If you're called to write, then you have something to say. And there's someone waiting to hear your words. You may not find your readers straight away, but they are out there. You've been given a gift. It's your duty to find the people who are ready to receive it.

That is what this book is about. It's about learning how to think, feel, and show up as the best writer you can be. How to do the work, even when it feels impossible. How to face uncertainty with courage so that you can experience the success you deserve.

There are thousands of resources that teach the specific steps to publish your book. The *how* of becoming an author is widely available information. I share my own process in another title, *Author Success Blueprint*. The book you're holding is something different.

This book provides the missing pieces to the puzzle. You don't need another writing or marketing tool. You aren't struggling because Amazon has changed its algorithm or because your genre has gone out of fashion.

If you want to take your writing career to the next level, you must harness the three habits of successful authors. Don't worry, the habits are quite straightforward. However, I'm not promising it will be easy. While understanding a thing can be simple, putting it into practice is a different matter. In this book, I will show you how.

What Creates Success

For a long time, I was obsessed with discovering the ingredients of success. I studied notable people across a variety of fields, including business, sports, and entertainment. I looked for common themes. I researched their backgrounds, habits, and characteristics. I wanted to know why only a tiny percentage of people succeeded in their chosen field.

At first, the answer eluded me. No two people followed the exact same path to success. But over time I noticed something interesting. I started to identify groups of habits. I played around with combining groups. I moved things around. I was working toward a framework for success.

Eventually, three types of habits emerged. At that point, I knew I was on to something. Three was a manageable number. This was a concept I had to share. But first I needed to test out my theory. I wanted to be sure the three habits worked.

Initially, I focused on the blogging world. Online business was an obvious place to start. Due to the low barriers to entry, there are many examples of successful bloggers—and many more examples of failed ones.

I interviewed 17 successful bloggers. Then I reviewed their answers and cross-checked them against the three habits. An exciting picture emerged: All the bloggers I met practiced the three habits. I shared the 17 interviews and wrote about my findings in my book, *The Essential Habits of 6-Figure Bloggers*.

But I didn't stop there. I turned my attention to my own business. I applied the habits to my career as an author. I also became certified as a life coach so that I could better understand how the human mind works. By this time, I knew how important it was to have the right mindset.

In 2019, my business grew exponentially. My author royalties increased from a few hundred a month to over $4,000. Other writers asked me to coach them so they could create similar results.

But not everyone can hire a coach. Which is where this book comes in. In these pages I teach you the three habits. I also share practical exercises so you can apply these concepts to your business and life. Follow the steps in this book and you can reach new levels in your writing career. I've done it and so have hundreds of my clients and readers. You can too.

The Three Habits

These habits aren't new. Gurus, coaches, philosophers, scientists, and spiritual teachers have all been teaching these ideas for centuries. What this book provides is a framework to help you sort through the mass of information, tools, and techniques to create your own version of success.

There are thousands of ways to apply each habit. Success for you won't look the same as it does for me or anyone else. The key is to implement each of the three habits by leveraging your unique strengths, experience, and values. This book gives you the steps to do exactly that.

The next thing you need to know is that you must practice all three habits. Many people are proficient in one or maybe even two. But that isn't enough. You need all three to reach your full potential.

Okay, here are the three habits:

1. *Act with purpose: Successful authors have a mission and take strategic action to fulfill their vision.*
2. *Create systems for success: Successful authors create systems so that essential tasks always get done.*
3. *Believe in yourself: Successful authors accept responsibility for their results and believe in their power to achieve the desired outcome, no matter what happens.*

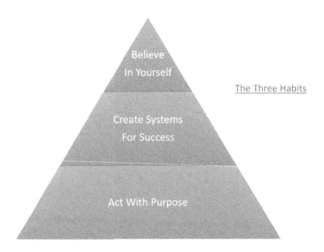

In chapter two, I describe each of the habits in more detail. Then, in the rest of this book, we explore practical tools you can use to implement these habits in your writing life.

Are you ready to level up your career as an author? If so, keep reading. You're about to discover the secrets of highly successful authors.

2

THE THREE HABITS

Why do some authors succeed, yet most do not? This is the question I answer in this book.

For every six- or seven-figure author, there are thousands who are struggling to make their first $1,000. According to the *Authors Guild 2018 Author Income Survey*, median incomes of all published authors surveyed was $6,080, down three percent from four years ago. This is not a full-time income.

The idea of the starving artist appears to be as true today as it was in the late 18th and early 19th centuries. Yet it doesn't have to be. In fact, if you want to join the ranks of highly paid authors, you must eliminate the concept of a starving artist from your mind.

Your first mission—should you choose to accept it—is to open your mind to the notion that anything is possible. I'm not asking you to instantly drop all your beliefs about what you can achieve as an author. That wouldn't be realistic. However, I am suggesting you at least consider the idea that you can earn six figures or more as a writer.

This is important. You can't make something happen if you don't believe in the possibility. Everything I teach you in this book works. But only if you trust that it will have the desired result for you.

In this chapter, I provide an overview of the three habits and how they fit together. I want you to understand the overall framework before you start practicing the individual pieces.

Habit 1: Act With Purpose

Here's the definition of habit one:

Successful authors have a mission and take strategic action to fulfill their vision.

There are two parts to this definition. First you need to have a mission. This is your purpose: the driving force that keeps you moving forward. A good mission is compelling to you. It fills you with excitement and fear. I describe how to define your purpose in chapter three.

Once you have a mission, you must take strategic action to fulfill your vision. This is the second part of habit one. At its simplest, this means having a plan and acting on it.

Now, your first plan may fail. So might your second, third, and fourth plans. Few people create the desired outcome on their first few attempts. History is littered with famous authors who failed many times before they became household names. J. K. Rowling received 12 rejection letters before a publisher accepted her first Harry Potter manuscript. Stephen King's book, *Carrie*, was rejected 30 times.

Imagine if these authors had given up after the first few setbacks. Failure is part of the process. Taking strategic action means you keep trying new things until you create the result you want. In chapters four and five, I show you how to formulate a strategy for your writing business. Then, in chapter six, we discuss how to act on it until you achieve success.

If you believe in the possibility, then you *can* create any outcome you want. Habit one tells us that to do this, you have to start by getting clear on your purpose. Then you must take strategic action to fulfill it.

Habit 2: Create Systems For Success

The second habit helps you follow through on your action plan. Here's the definition:

Successful authors create systems so that essential tasks always get done.

You can have a solid approach and still fail. You can take courses, learn from experts, and map out a path to success, yet never meet your goals. Maybe life gets in the way or you don't see results fast enough. This is when many of us throw in the towel.

But, as we've already established, failure is part of the process. Successful authors don't give up. They keep going in the face of obstacles. And here's their secret: They don't rely on willpower alone. Instead, they utilize systems to ensure the work always gets done.

Systems are not limited to computers or software. They include daily rituals, outsourcing work, batching related tasks, and more. A system is anything that automates the strategic activities in habit one.

In section two of this book, we discuss the three types of systems used by successful authors. You will learn how to create a writing habit, publishing process, and marketing system.

This is the bottom line: Unless you're superhuman, you need systems to stay consistent and succeed. Don't rely on willpower alone to achieve your goals. Willpower is a limited resource. At some point, you will not be able to sustain the effort. Whereas, with solid systems in place, essential tasks are always completed.

Habit 3: Believe In Yourself

Lastly, we come to the most important habit of all. This is the one I have struggled with the most. It's the reason why I became certified as a coach. I wanted to master my own mindset and create new results in my life, then help others do the same.

Anyone can follow a blueprint or a strategy, but not everyone gets the same outcome. The final difference between people who succeed and people who give up is how they manage the mind. Successful authors overcome the limitations of the human brain to reach their full potential.

Here is the definition of habit three:

Successful authors accept responsibility for their results and believe in their power to achieve the desired outcome, no matter what happens.

Actively working on this habit transforms your writing career. Let's unpack the definition so you can truly grasp how habit three works. It has three parts:

1. "Successful authors accept responsibility for their results" means adopting a no excuses mindset. When something unexpected happens—which it will—you get to decide how to respond. You can blame outside events or you can change what you're thinking and doing. Top performers understand that they, and they alone, are responsible for their results.

2. Successful authors "believe in their power to achieve the desired outcome." We all carry a set of fears and beliefs. Some of our beliefs hold us back. Habit three means not letting negative thoughts and recurring stories limit your achievement. Instead, you must believe in yourself and your mission.

3. Finally, "no matter what happens" means doing it scared. We're all afraid and we all encounter obstacles. To find success you must lean into your fear and keep moving forward, even when faced with seemingly insurmountable setbacks.

Of the three habits, the third is the most overlooked. It's also the hardest to conquer. Many people focus on strategy and tactics, adopting new tools or following the latest trend. But, strategy and tactics will only get you so far.

Fortunately, there are many ways to strengthen your belief. In the final section of this book I describe the tools my coaching clients and I have found most helpful. I show you how to believe in yourself and how to act no matter what comes up. You will learn how to believe in any possibility so you can make your dreams a reality.

SECTION ONE
HABIT ONE: ACT WITH PURPOSE

3

WHY YOU WRITE

Recently, I watched the movie *Neil Armstrong*. Much of the movie focused on Armstrong's role in the first moon landing. I was fascinated by the detailed planning that went into the Apollo 11 space mission. The astronauts underwent an intense six-month training for a mission that lasted just over eight days. Every aspect of the journey was mapped out and practiced in advance.

Writing a book is not the same as completing a space mission. However, starting with a blueprint greatly increases your chances of succeeding. You can't get where you want to go without knowing how to get there. Habit one shows you how to adopt a strategy that fits you and your aspirations.

The habits are all important. You won't reach your full potential as an author unless you practice all three. However, habit one is where you must start. Even if you already have a goal and strategy for your author career, I encourage you to read these initial chapters. Make sure you have a firm grasp on the first habit before addressing the other two.

Here's a reminder of the definition of habit one:

Successful authors have a mission and take strategic action to fulfill their vision.

There are two elements to this definition. First, you need a personal mission. Second, you need to follow a proven strategy to achieve your goals and fulfill your purpose.

In this chapter, we define your personal mission or purpose.

Why You Need a Purpose

Having a purpose keeps you motivated. As a writer, you experience struggle. Finishing your book is a grind. You question the quality of your work. You worry that nobody will read your book. Or worse, they will hate it and leave scathing reviews. Having a purpose is the antidote that keeps you going through the difficult times.

Here are some signs that you don't yet have a clear purpose as an author:

You don't feel excited about your writing.

You don't feel connected to your readers or future readers.

You struggle to find things to write about.

You don't enjoy the writing process.

You don't know what to do to sell more books.

You don't know how to make money selling your books.

You don't have enough time to work as an author.

You find you start writing books, but you never finish a manuscript.

If any of these statements ring true for you, then you're not alone. All writers experience self-doubt. Believing you're called to write does not grant you immunity to negative thoughts and emotions. In this chapter, I share the first step to handling your fear. In section three, we discuss additional tools to manage your mindset.

There's a second reason why having a purpose is important. It helps you sell more books.

When you know your purpose, everything about your book appeals to your target readers. Your mission informs the way you write and package your book. Packaging includes the title, subtitle, cover, and text on the back of your book. Your packaging must appeal directly to your ideal readers. The clearer you are on who those people are and why you're writing for them, the more your book will speak to them.

In summary, when you connect with your readers and your purpose, you make a greater impact. You overcome fear, create your best work, sell more books, and earn higher royalties.

Common Reasons To Write

Before defining your mission, it's helpful to understand why you want to be an author. Below are six common reasons why people write books. As you read through these options, listen to your feelings. Which ideas resonate with you? Which ones might be part of your purpose?

Be honest with yourself. There's no right or wrong answer. You don't need to share your thoughts with anybody else. This is personal to you. Look for reasons that generate strong positive emotions.

1. Earn Royalties

Perhaps you want to earn passive income. This is quite possible as an author. The work to create and launch your book is a one-time effort. You then receive royalties every month your book is available in stores or online. Of course, you need to write a book people want to read and launch it effectively. We discuss how to do this in subsequent chapters.

I still receive a small monthly check for the first book I published in

2015. I spend little to no time marketing this title. As an author, you create assets that keep earning you income long after you publish your book.

2. Gain Instant Authority

When you publish a nonfiction book, you instantly establish yourself as an expert in your niche.

This happened to me by accident. After I wrote my first book, *Make Money on Airbnb,* I was approached by people who wanted my opinion on Airbnb hosting. I also landed a high paying freelance writing gig for an Airbnb company, and I was invited to speak at several conferences for Airbnb hosts.

Unfortunately, I didn't want to become an Airbnb expert, so I turned down most of these opportunities. But I did learn a valuable lesson. Ever since this happened, I have been more deliberate about publishing books which help establish my authority in the work-from-home niche. This strategy has helped me sell online courses, sign four-figure coaching clients, be invited to speak at online conferences, and more.

If you want to quickly establish yourself as an expert, for example as a consultant or a coach, then publishing a book helps you do that.

3. Grow Your Following

Every title you put into the world has the potential to grow your email list or social media following. This is important for both fiction and nonfiction writers. You need to build up a following of readers who love your work. This helps you sell more books or other products and services in the future.

Most of my coaching clients find me through my books. When I take stock of the business growth I've experienced since first hitting the publish button, I realize that writing books has been the savviest decision in my career with the highest return on investment.

Here's how it works. First, decide what bonus you want to offer. Make sure it's irresistible to your ideal readers, provides immediate results, and cannot be easily included in your book. Examples include audio, video, spreadsheet, or an online reader community.

Next, create your bonus and an email sign-up form. This is the form or page you link to in your book. Make sure you deliver the bonuses when someone subscribes via the email sign-up form. To do this, you need to open an account with an email service provider. Then set up an email that is automatically sent when a person subscribes. In your welcome email, deliver your bonus or tell people where they can find it.

In this post, I walk readers through the technical steps to create an email sign-up form and welcome email using ConvertKit: sallyann-miller.com/grow-your-email-list-convertkit. Other popular email service providers are MailerLite and MailChimp.

Finally, insert links to your bonus sign-up form inside your book. I suggest you create a dedicated bonus page. You can find an example bonus page at the start of this book. Then, insert five to ten additional links within appropriate chapters. Be careful not to include too many, as this can annoy readers.

4. Spread a Message

Do you have a message you want to share with the world? When you publish a book on Amazon you have the potential to reach millions of people around the globe.

One of my coaching clients, Stephanie Johnson, writes and illustrates social-emotional children's books. Her mission is to teach children to look inside themselves for the strength and courage to thrive. She is passionate about showing young people the capable and talented individuals they are.

Stephanie's mission keeps her motivated and drives her to extraordinary lengths to sell her books. She is leveraging her books and the Amazon platform to spread a message she cares about. You can read more about how she got started as a children's author on my blog: sallyannmiller.com/sell-more-books/

5. Teach Something

Publishing a nonfiction book is one way you can help a lot of people. There is no ongoing maintenance, like there is with an online course or a coaching program. Once you hit the publish button, there's a potential for millions of people to learn from your experience and expertise.

For example, my make money from home books teach people different ways they can earn an income from home. These are step-by-step guides that help people go from zero to profitable. I have published books for bloggers, coaches, writers, freelancers, personal trainers, and more.

If you want to teach through your books, make sure you hold nothing back. Give your readers everything they need to achieve the promised outcome. A well-written how-to book breaks bigger problems into smaller steps, and then shows the reader how to complete each action item until they realize the desired result.

6. Get Published

Finally, publishing a book may be a bucket list item for you. You have always dreamed about writing a book. You're ready to finally call yourself a published author.

If you resonate with this reason, be honest with yourself. Wanting to try something new is a valid motivator. This is the real reason why I wrote my first book. I wanted to see if I could do it. I only realized the other benefits many months after I first published.

But be warned, you may discover you love the world of writing and publishing. That first book might set you on the path to becoming a full-time author!

Your Personal Mission Statement

Okay, now you have a sense for why you want to write. Let's get more specific and create your personal mission statement.

Remember, connecting to your purpose helps you stay focused and motivated over the long haul. In the action steps, I share an exercise to help you write a mission statement that feels true to you. Your goal is to define a vision that fuels action in your business.

You know you've nailed your mission statement when the feelings associated with your purpose are greater than any discomfort you might experience in your writing career. For example, I have a mission to sell a million books that help people live better lives. My mission inspires me when I want to give up. It helps me keep going through the good and the bad. It also scares me a little.

A great mission statement should require you to grow into a new version of yourself, which is something you must do in order to face things you've never tried before and overcome fear and doubt. If you're not scared, then your purpose isn't big enough.

When you think about your purpose, you might feel inspiration, excitement, enthusiasm, commitment, determination, or any other positive feeling. The emotion is personal to you. The key is to tap into a feeling that compels you to take extraordinary action. The emotion that drives your work determines the results you create. This is a key concept, and one we'll return to in chapter fourteen.

Action Steps

1. Review the six common reasons to write listed in this chapter. What will writing do for you and your family?

2. Now think about your bigger vision for your life and your writing career. In a journal, answer the following questions. (NOTE: These questions are influenced by Todd Henry's book *Louder Than Words*)

When are you at your best? When do others respond most to your ideas? What are your unique strengths?

When are you moved emotionally? When can you recall getting emotional about something you experienced? Why were you moved?

What stirs you to compassionate anger? When do you get angry on behalf of someone else who has been wronged?

What gives you great hope? When have you taken a position, even in the face of skepticism or criticism from others?

What kind of problems are you naturally drawn to solving? What are the qualities of these problems?

3. Review your answers above. Look for problems you're drawn to solve, people you're moved to help, positive change you want to see in the world. We all have themes, movements, ideas which ignite us. What moves you? Think in terms of who you want to help and what you want to do for them. In your journal, write out your personal mission.

Here're some real-world mission statements to inspire you:

Headspace: "To improve the health and happiness of the world."

HEIFER International (non-profit): "To work with communities to end world hunger and poverty and to care for the Earth."

Microsoft: "To empower every person and every organization on the planet to achieve more."

Virgin Atlantic Airways: "To embrace the human spirit and let it fly."

Sally Miller: "To sell 1,000,000 books that help people live a better life."

4. Take a break for a day or two. Then read the mission statement you created in step three. Ask yourself:

- Does it clearly communicate the specific outcome or change you want to create?

- Does it capture what you most want from your writing career?
- How does it make you feel when you imagine each outcome becoming a reality?

The best mission statements both excite and scare you. If you aren't at least a little afraid, then it's not big enough. This is your life's work. Make sure it stretches you to your fullest.

If you need to, add or change details until your purpose is well-defined and creates a strong emotional response. In the upcoming chapters, we explore how to take strategic action so you can bring your writing dreams to life.

4

AUTHOR BUSINESS STRATEGY

You have a personal mission, one that inspires and scares you. In the next three chapters, I show you how to live your purpose. This is the second part of habit one. You must take strategic action to fulfill your vision.

We begin by discussing your high-level business strategy. As an author you have some key decisions to make that will determine your overall direction. You don't have to make these choices when starting out. I didn't. However, if I'd been more deliberate in my business, then my career as an author would have advanced much more quickly.

If you're seeking to maximize your success, take some time to plot your journey now. You can always change course as you go. These decisions are not intended to lock you into one path for the remainder of your writing career.

Self-Publishing Versus Traditional Publishing

First, decide whether to pursue traditional publishing, self-publishing, or a hybrid of the two. I'm a self-published author and so I may be a little biased here. I like flexibility and as an independent author you create a business on your own terms.

However, there are disadvantages to self-publishing, and I'd be remiss not to spell them out. Independent authors must wear many hats. You aren't just a writer; you are also a publisher and marketer. You own the process of getting your book into stores and letting people know it exists. There are a lot of skills you need to master. You spend at least half your time doing activities other than writing.

Whereas, if you're a traditionally published author, someone else takes care of the publishing process. This includes editing, cover design, distribution to bookstores, collection of royalties, and more. You might also receive an advance, depending on the publisher, which means you may not have to wait until your book sells before you get paid.

However, traditional publishing is a slower process. It can take up to two years or more between writing your book and seeing it on bookshelves. Also, publishers still expect you to get involved in the marketing process. The time spent building and engaging a reader following is the same regardless of the route you select.

The biggest downsides of traditional publishing are loss of royalties and control. It is essential you understand any publishing agreement you sign. You may be required to give away your rights to your work for a certain period of time, depending on the contract. You also give up a large percentage of royalties to the publishing house.

It used to be the case that being traditionally published carried more prestige. However, this is less true as the self-publishing industry has matured. Most readers don't care—or even know—how your book appeared in the store. All they want is an enjoyable reading experience.

Finally, you can follow a hybrid route, which means taking a different approach for each book. Perhaps you want to self-publish your popular fiction series, but you have a title in a different genre that you'd like to see picked up by a traditional publisher.

If you're struggling to decide between self-publishing and traditional publishing, refer back to your mission statement. Which route best supports your mission and the reasons why you want to write?

Author Business Models

Within the writing world, there are hundreds of ways to structure your career. Below is an overview of the most common business models. As you read them, think about what kind of writer you want to be. Decide how you want to spend most of your time. Select a model that fits your purpose and plays to your strengths.

Of course, you can also make up your own business model. Design a life and career you want—not what other people tell you to do. This is not a fixed set of options. Take what appeals to you and feel free to mix and match ideas.

Model #1: The Writer

You simply want to write. You publish at least three books a year. In the case of fiction, you may publish 10 or more books every year.

This is the most straightforward business model.

Your income is 100 percent from book royalties. You spend all your time writing, publishing, and promoting your books.

Model #2: The Mega Bestseller

You poured everything into writing one book, and now it's a bestseller. You have no desire to write any more books (unless you can pay a ghostwriter to create them for you).

After publishing, you spend most of your time marketing your one book. You love marketing.

Your income is at least 80 percent book royalties on one title. You may have some other income from other sources, such as speaking or coaching, but these avenues are not part of your main focus.

Model #3: The Coach or Consultant Who Enjoys Writing

You're an online business owner—probably a coach or consultant—who also likes to write. You publish one or more books with the specific goal of growing your business. Your book is a source of leads and gives you increased authority in your field.

You spend less than 20 percent of your time writing and marketing books. Most of your time is spent on your other business activities. Less than 20 percent of your income comes from book royalties.

The Hybrid Business

You may not fit precisely into any of these models. I don't! I am somewhere between models one and three, depending on where my current interests lie.

Don't let these options restrict you. Instead, understand where you want your income to come from. This tells you where to focus your time. I discuss income sources in more detail below.

Multiple Streams Of Income

As an author, you can earn money from a diverse range of sources. The most obvious is book royalties. But even within this category, there are many ways to increase your earnings from one title. The following is a summary of the most common types of author income. As with your business model, don't let these choices restrict you. Nor should you become distracted from your main purpose to write books. Instead, note the ideas that interest you, then plan to incorporate them into your career.

Book Royalties

You can publish in several different formats—eBook, paperback, audiobook, or large print. You can also make your book available in multiple channels including online and offline bookstores, libraries, and book subscription services. Finally, you can either sell the foreign rights to your book or have it translated yourself.

By doing these things, you create multiple assets from a single title.

Each asset increases your chances of reaching a new reader base and earning more income.

Affiliate Sales

You can also make money as an affiliate for other people's products.

When you sign up for an affiliate program, you receive an affiliate link. You can place this link on your website, in your emails, or in your eBooks (though make sure you familiarize yourself with the program's terms and conditions). Every time someone clicks on the link and makes a purchase, you earn a commission on the sale. There is no additional cost to the customer.

Online Products

Perhaps you are not comfortable promoting someone else's products, or maybe you feel you can create something better that your audience will love. If this is the case, go for it! These next income sources are all about selling your own products and services.

For example, you can create a training program that goes deeper into your book topic. There are many ways to create and sell a training program. You can leverage an existing platform that already has thousands of course buyers. Udemy is one such platform.

Alternatively, you can deliver your course via your own website. Some ways to do this are:

> An email course. For this, you need an email service that has autoresponder or drip feed functionality.

> An eBook sold from your website using a PayPal button or via a service like Gumroad.

> A course built on an all-in-one platform such as Teachable or Podia.

> A self-hosted video course on your own website. You can use a WordPress plugin like WishList Member.

Workshops and Events

You may prefer to connect in-person with your readers. In this case, you can create workshops or events. This could be a ten-person seminar at your local church or a thousand-person conference at a large hotel. Other ideas include a retreat or workshop.

One-On-One Service

Another option is to offer a one-on-one service. These can be high value and are ideal if you are called to help people at a personal level.

Many nonfiction authors offer a coaching service that relates to their topic. If coaching is not your thing, you can provide a different type of service. For example, I used to offer a website review service. I helped people convert website visitors into email subscribers and customers. I presented my clients with a 15-minute video and a written report of my recommendations.

Speaking

Lastly, you can seek opportunities to get paid as a speaker. For many, speaking is immensely rewarding. It's also an effective way to reach a new book-buying audience. This is what Marcy Pusey did when she visited California for a friend's wedding.

Marcy was invited to speak at an Orphan Care Summit as the close-out speaker. She brought along copies of her recently published book, *Reclaiming Hope*. At the event, Marcy sold every physical copy she had with her and more. During her trip, she earned $600 in physical book sales.

Marcy told me, "Having a published book opens doors. It gives you a professional voice and credibility."

Exclusive Versus Wide

If you are self-publishing, your final decision is whether to stay exclusive with Amazon or publish wide.

I stayed exclusive to Amazon for my first four years. In early 2020, I started experimenting with publishing my books wide. So, I have personal experience with both solutions. Below I outline the pros and cons of the two options. As you read through the pros and cons, keep your mission statement in mind. Also consider where you currently are in your writing business. Are you a newbie or do you already have some experience in the publishing world? How many resources do you want to commit to writing versus publishing?

There's no one right way to self-publish your book. It all depends on your personal and professional goals.

Exclusive To Amazon – Pros

More books are sold on Amazon than on all the other platforms combined. Okay, this is a bold statement and a statistic that's difficult to verify. Figuring out Amazon's exact market share is close to impossible given just how many places you can buy books worldwide and the unreliability of the available sales data. But based on anecdotal evidence (and what data is out there) most indie authors make at least half of their royalties from Amazon.

Publishing on just Amazon is a lot less work. You only need to learn one platform, format your book once, and view your royalties in one place. Consolidating your reviews and sales in one place—instead of spreading them across multiple sites—can also help you climb further up the Amazon bestseller lists.

When you're exclusive with Amazon, you can enroll your book in KDP Select. This allows you to run Kindle Countdown Deals and Free Book Promotions which can help you sell more books. Having your book in KDP Select also means your book is available in Kindle Unlimited (Amazon's book subscription program). This helps you reach more readers. There are some people who only read eBooks via Kindle Unlimited.

Finally, if you enroll in KDP Select, your book typically has a higher Amazon Ranking and this can help even more readers discover your book. When I pulled my books from KDP Select, I saw a significant fall in ranking, but an increase in royalties made up for it. I make around $3.40 every time I sell a $4.99 eBook, BUT only around 60 cents on a KU borrow of the same book (depending on how many pages the KU borrower reads).

Exclusive To Amazon – Cons

When you're exclusive you miss out on readers who buy their books elsewhere. For example, Apple Books, Google Play, Kobo, Barnes & Noble and even local bookstores. You also lose the opportunity to get your book into libraries (both physical and online).

Exclusivity means you put all your eggs in one basket. If Amazon ever changes their algorithm or their rules, you could be vulnerable. This is the main driver for my decision to publish my books wide.

Some authors object to the fact that Amazon has so much control and argue that you're not truly independent if you depend on Amazon for your livelihood. I'm more of a realist. I focus my efforts where my readers are, and I see the most benefit. If that means selling most of my books through Amazon, then I'm okay with that.

Publish Wide – Pros

When you publish wide, you reach more readers and more countries. Not everybody buys their books on Amazon. You can publish your book in multiple online and offline stores, libraries, and subscription services like Scribd.

By diversifying across multiple platforms, you reduce your risk of being negatively impacted by changes on one platform. You also support the smaller publishing platforms who are struggling to take on the "giant" of online selling (aka Amazon).

Finally, there can be some prestige attached to having your books widely available.

Publish Wide – Cons

There's additional work when you publish across multiple platforms. This was the main reason I held back for so long. When publishing wide you must manage multiple formats, platforms, and income sources. It was difficult to justify the extra effort for what may be a small impact on my total book sales.

When you're no longer exclusive, Amazon won't let you enroll in Kindle Select. And so you lose out on the opportunity to reach Kindle Unlimited readers, boost your Amazon ranking, and run KDP Select sales.

So what should you do? Here's my take on this debate.

If you want to reach a lot of readers for the least amount of overhead, then publish exclusively on Amazon. I still believe going exclusive is best for first-time authors who are figuring out the publishing world. You can always widen your reach once you have a handle on Amazon's platform and algorithm.

Being exclusive is also an accepted strategy for indie authors who write specifically for Kindle Unlimited readers. These authors build up a large KU following and publish a high volume of books in a narrowly defined fiction genre.

However, if you have the time to experiment and want to have your book available in as many places as possible, then go "wide." This is what I'm doing, but only after four happy years of exclusivity.

Action Steps

1. Decide whether you wish to publish independently or through traditional means.

2. Review the business models discussed in this chapter and determine which is the best fit for your personal mission.

3. If you want to earn income in addition to book royalties, review the different streams of income and select one or two that will help you fulfill your personal mission.

4. Decide whether to publish exclusively on Amazon or across multiple retail outlets.

These steps involve a lot of decisions. If you're a new author, you may be feeling overwhelmed. Take a deep breath and relax. The choices you make now can always be changed in the future. Focus on your personal mission and keep moving. You can do this.

In the next two chapters, I show you how to set and achieve extraordinary goals. You will discover why most goals don't work and how to create more success in your writing business than you thought possible.

5

SET EXTRAORDINARY GOALS

There's something magical about starting a new year. It's the perfect time to dream and to remember anything is possible in your life. It doesn't matter if you didn't meet your goals for the previous year. It's okay if you didn't start your business. Or didn't make as much money as you hoped. Because this is a fresh start. This is your chance to have an extraordinary year.

But why wait for a new year before changing your life? There's nothing mysterious about January first. You can tap into that same excitement right now. You don't need to wait to start imagining a new future for yourself.

That's what this chapter is about. You have a purpose for your writing business. It's time to start living into that vision.

An Extraordinary Life

Your extraordinary life begins with setting an extraordinary goal. I've tried various goal setting systems, and I've had mixed results.

Then in 2019, I had the most extraordinary year of my life. I lost 25 pounds in weight. I tripled the size of my business. And I worked just

15 to 20 hours every week. I'm now working toward a six-figure writing income, just from my book royalties. Ultimately, it's my mission to sell more than one million books.

A few years ago, I wouldn't have dared dream so big. It never crossed my mind that this would be possible for me. I thought writing books meant earning a small income. I believed that to make six figures as an author, I'd have to build a big business and work long hours.

So, what changed? I learned to set and achieve extraordinary goals. I believe I can accomplish anything. In this chapter and the next one, I teach you how you can do the same.

An extraordinary goal isn't like other goals. It's the kind of goal that creates extraordinary results and changes your life. However, an extraordinary goal isn't just a big goal. It's more than that. An extraordinary goal meets three criteria. It's measurable, meaningful, and evokes a strong emotional reaction.

The first criteria is your goal must be measurable. I've set goals that aren't measurable before and it doesn't work. When you can't measure something, you can't monitor your progress. And when you can't evaluate your forward movement, you have no way of knowing what else you need to do to achieve your goal.

Here are some examples of measurable goals:

Make $100,000 gross income in one year.

Earn $5,000/month in gross income.

Have 5,000 email subscribers.

Sell 20,000 copies of your book.

However, be careful not to use metrics in your business as an excuse to feel badly if you think you're advancing too slowly. The only reason to measure your progress is so you can make data-driven decisions. We discuss how to evaluate your results in the next chapter.

Making your goal measurable isn't enough. Extraordinary goals must also be meaningful to you. On your business journey, you will encounter obstacles. When you care deeply about your work, it's easier to keep going through the tough times.

A meaningful goal is one that ties back to your personal mission statement. By working toward your goal, you are living your purpose. For example, if your goal is to earn a certain income, think about how the extra money will change your life. In what way will it help you fulfill your mission?

Perhaps you want to be an example of what's possible as an author, or maybe you want to help other people create change in their lives. Or maybe you simply want to do the kind of work that lights you up.

If you're struggling to come up with a meaningful goal that's also measurable, then try thinking about it this way. Money—or any other metric—is just a measurement of your progress. You don't need to find meaning in the number. It's neutral information, and simply a way to determine whether or not you're moving closer to fulfilling your mission statement.

Finally, extraordinary goals evoke a mix of excitement and fear. We discussed this in the previous chapter when you set your mission statement. The fear part is important. If you're not afraid when you think about your goal, then it's either too small or too big.

Goals that are too small don't scare you because you already know how to achieve them. And if you know how to achieve them but haven't done so, then they aren't meaningful enough to you.

On the flip side, goals that are too big don't scare you because you don't believe they are possible. I call these fantasy goals. A fantasy goal is when you want to have a million-dollar business but haven't yet earned your first dollar. It's like dreaming about winning the lottery. It's fun to think about, but your brain doesn't think it will happen. And so, there's no fear involved.

It's All About the Journey

One final thought on goals. Don't set goals because you think your life will improve when you reach the finishing line. If you're constantly chasing the result, then you're missing out on the experience of making it happen.

Your life won't instantly improve the moment you achieve your goal. There will still be good and bad in your world. You may have reached one goal, but your brain will find a new set of problems to tackle.

The point of setting an extraordinary goal is the person you become as you pursue it. The skills you master. The experiences you enjoy. The self-confidence you generate. The change you create in the world.

Once you understand this, it doesn't matter whether you achieve your goal or not. Either way, you are embracing an extraordinary life.

Action Steps

1. Brainstorm what you want to achieve over the next 12 months in your writing business. Remember, the best goals have a measurable outcome. For example: earn $50,000 in your business, sell 10,000 copies of your book.

2. Now, review your goal and make sure it meets the following criteria:

- It's specific and measurable.
- It's meaningful to you, and it brings you closer to fulfilling your personal mission.
- It fills you with excitement AND fear.
- You don't yet know how to fulfill your goal.

If you're not at least a little scared, then your goal is too small. And if you already know how to fulfill your goal, then it isn't extraordinary enough. If you need to, adjust your goal by making it bigger.

An extraordinary goal requires you to become a new person in order to achieve it. You acquire new skills, knowledge, or experience on your way to fulfilling your mission. Working toward an extraordinary goal means doing things you've never done before to create an extraordinary result in the world. This drives you to act with purpose.

In the next chapter, I show you how to create and execute a plan to achieve your extraordinary goal. This is the final tool you need to master the first habit of successful authors.

6

ACHIEVE YOUR GOALS

Have you set an extraordinary goal? Does it fit with your personal mission? Is your brain freaking out right now?

If you answer yes to all three questions, then you're doing this right. As soon as you set your extraordinary goal, your brain presents you with all the reasons why you should give up. If it doesn't, then your goal isn't big enough. In which case, I want you to revisit chapter five and create a new goal. One that scares you, as well as excites you.

Your next step is to create a plan and act on it. Remember, habit one tells us that successful authors take strategic action to fulfill their vision. A goal without action is just a dream.

Are you ready? There are five steps in this chapter:

1. Brainstorm Tasks

2. Anticipate Obstacles

3. Create a Plan

4. Follow Through

5. Evaluate Results

Brainstorm Tasks

Start by breaking your extraordinary goal into a series of smaller goals. Planning an entire year can be overwhelming, and you may feel less urgency to follow through. Your brain tricks you into believing there's plenty of time to get the work done, which can lead to procrastination.

I like to plan three months at a time. For example, if your extraordinary goal is to sell 10,000 books in the next 12 months, then your first three-month goal might be to publish one book.

The result of completing your extraordinary action must be concrete —something nobody can argue about. It's also important to have a deadline and a way of measuring whether you're moving in the right direction. For example, the three-month goal to publish one book can be stated as follows:

I will have published my book [Title] by [Date]. I will know I have achieved this result because my book will be available for purchase on Amazon.

Next, it's time to brainstorm everything you need to do to accomplish this outcome. Don't worry about what you don't know (we will cover that in the next step). Focus on what you do know.

Your brain may not want to do this exercise. It will try to convince you that you don't know how to achieve your goal. I ask you to trust yourself. Your brain is resourceful. It's your job to unlock the power you have hidden within.

Write down all the tasks you can think of to help you accomplish your goal. Let your mind come up with as many ideas as possible. At this stage, don't try to organize activities into a sequence. In future steps, you will fill in any gaps and create a timeline. For now, get everything you can out of your brain and onto paper.

Anticipate Obstacles

In a previous life, I managed complex software projects. At the start of each project, we were required to write a contingency plan. First, we would identify any events that might prevent us from completing the project on time and in budget. Then we would create a plan to handle these events if they occurred. We planned ahead of time for all the things that could go wrong.

If you can anticipate obstacles in advance, you can find solutions. In fact, the obstacles are the strategy. On the way to achieving anything new, there are going to be problems. As Roman Emperor Marcus Aurelius once said:

"The impediment to action advances action. What stands in the way becomes the way."

This is what separates successful authors from those who fail. Successful authors see obstacles and embrace the challenge. They know the desired result is on the other side of the obstacle.

Many of the obstacles that stand between you and success are created in your mind. Your brain wants to rebel against doing anything new or difficult. In this step, I want you to give your fearful mind free rein. Rather than suppress your doubts, get them out into the open. When you do that, you can start preparing for potential obstacles instead of avoiding them.

In your journal, write out all the reasons why your goal is difficult. Do not judge your thoughts. Your brain is designed to see all the things that can go wrong. It wants to keep you safe and it does this by convincing you to abandon challenging situations.

Bring all your doubts to the surface. Dig deep. Hold nothing back. Let it ALL out. Don't be afraid to investigate the murky corners. I promise you, there's no thought in your head that millions of other authors haven't already had.

Here are some common obstacles writers face:

I don't know how to write a book.

Working on my book will take time away from my kids.

I'm not a good enough writer.

I don't know what to write about.

My spouse and friends will laugh at me.

Next, create a plan to handle each obstacle that's standing between you and your goal. Your brain may rebel further during this step. I want you to open yourself up to possibility. Your mind is powerful. Redirect it toward finding solutions instead of problems.

One way to do this is by imagining you are the person who has already accomplished your goal. Review each obstacle you wrote down and ask how you overcame it. Some of your strategies will be new thoughts to practice. We dive deeper into how to manage your thinking in section three of this book. Here are some example obstacles and strategies:

I don't know how to write a book. -> I will take a writing course and follow all the action steps to finish my book.

Working on my book will take time away from my kids. -> I will work on my book between five a.m. and seven a.m. before my kids wake up.

I'm not a good enough writer. -> I will practice this thought every day: "I'm becoming a better writer."

Create A Plan

By now you should have a list of tasks and strategies to achieve your goal. Next, I want you to schedule everything on a calendar. Yes, everything. You can use any calendar tool, whether it's a paper planner or Google calendar. The key to using your calendar effectively is to set appointments with yourself for all the tasks you need to do.

Start by blocking out leisure time such as your workout, lunch break, family time, and more. Also, create time slots for recurring activities. These are activities you do every day or week. This may include checking and replying to emails and voicemails, book-keeping tasks, client appointments, or scheduling social media posts.

You should now have a clear picture of how much time you have available to work on your goal. You may find that you only have 30 minutes open each day. That was my situation when I wrote my first book. I had a preschooler and a new baby at home. There was little free time for writing and building my business. I didn't let this stop me. I accepted that my progress would be gradual and focused on what I could do rather than what I could not.

Taking an honest look at how much time you have to work on your goal prevents you from over-scheduling yourself and burning out. Once you've established your availability, review the action items you identified in the previous two steps. Place them in the order they need to happen. Finally, determine how much time each task will take and assign them to your calendar.

It's worth repeating. Your brain is likely to come up with excuses as you create your plan. It will tell you that you don't know how long a task will take. Or that the process is too difficult. These are all attempts to derail you. Thank your brain and keep going. Put everything onto your calendar.

You now have an action plan to achieve your goal.

Follow Through

Once you have your calendar set up, you must follow through. This is the hardest part.

Acting on your plan means saying no to non-urgent tasks that aren't on your calendar. Working on tasks, even when you don't feel like it. Completing activities in the time you have allotted for them.

The secret to mastering these skills is two-fold. First, you must be aware when your brain is making excuses. Second, you must follow through anyway. As you learn to honor your calendar, you build trust with yourself. This is how you become the kind of person who gets things done.

Below is a weekly process you can use to help you honor your calendar and achieve your goals.

1. Once a week, review the tasks on your calendar. I do this on Sunday night. It takes approximately 15 minutes to plan the next seven days and it saves me hours of time during the week.

2. If necessary, adjust your calendar so you have time scheduled for everything that needs to happen this week. If you have too many tasks, ask yourself this question: "What tasks will move me closest to achieving my goal?" Discard any unimportant tasks.

3. Then, show up to each appointment on your calendar. If you're doing focused work, clear off your desk, shut down your Internet browser and social media. And if your brain wants you to do something else, acknowledge it. Then gently remind yourself that you are going to do the work anyway. This is a daily practice, so don't give up. You are learning how to follow through.

4. Work (without interruption) on your task for the entire appointment time. Do not stop to answer the phone, do not check your email and do not allow others to distract you. Shut your door if you can.

Following through is not easy. Not only are you learning how to act when you don't want to, you're also opening yourself up to failure. The plan you create won't always generate the desired outcome. This is where the last step comes in. You must evaluate your results.

Evaluate Results

Achieving any goal is an iterative process. Few authors find success right out of the gate. You must constantly analyze your progress and look for ways to improve. If you're prepared to keep testing and improving, then success is inevitable.

Don't keep taking the same action if it isn't working. You must tweak your plan based on feedback. I suggest you evaluate your results every week. Write down your answers to the following questions:

1. What did I do this week? Write out the specific action steps you took.

2. What was the outcome of this action? Describe the results of your action. List the positive results first. Don't allow your brain to focus only on the undesirable outcomes. For example, number of words you wrote, number of books sold, dollars earned, etc. Include numbers wherever possible.

3. How can I improve next week? Describe all the ways you think you might be able to improve on your results and move closer to your extraordinary goal.

You must be prepared to keep testing and be open to failure. If you're willing to fail as many times as it takes, then success is guaranteed.

Action Steps

Follow the four steps in this chapter to create a plan to achieve your extraordinary goal. Then start acting on it.

1. Brainstorm Tasks

2. Anticipate Obstacles

3. Create a Plan

4. Follow Through

5. Evaluate Results

The system described in this chapter helps eliminate stress. When you feel overwhelmed, step back and repeat the five steps. Stop trying to hold your to-do list in your head or on scraps of paper. Instead, put everything onto your calendar and start following through.

The process I taught you in this chapter is simple. But of course, it can be challenging to put into practice. If there's a day when you don't honor your schedule, be kind to yourself. Then decide to get back on track the next day. In the next section, I share more tools to help you follow through. You will discover how successful authors always get the work done, no matter what happens.

SECTION TWO

HABIT TWO: CREATE SYSTEMS FOR SUCCESS

7

BECOMING SUPERHUMAN

My son is obsessed with superheroes. One of his favorite games is to ask this question:

"If you could have any superpower, what would it be?"

The usual answers include flying, super strength, and lightning speed. Of course, these are all powers we're unlikely to attain. And the truth is they wouldn't be useful in the real world. However, you can still surpass your current human limitations, and you don't need a superpower to do it. In this chapter, I show you how.

Imagine knowing you will achieve anything you set out to do. This is the power of the second habit. Habit two tells us that successful authors create systems to ensure essential tasks are always completed. In the previous chapter, you implemented your first process. You created a plan to achieve your extraordinary goal. You also learned how to follow through on your plan.

In the next four chapters, you will create further systems so you can accomplish much more in your writing career.

What Is a System?

When I Googled the word "system," here's what I found:

A system is a set of principles or procedures, according to which something is done; an organized framework or method.

This definition tells us that a system is a way to accomplish something in a repeatable and consistent manner. A system does this by automating the steps to generate a defined outcome.

Some systems are automated with technology. One example is an email sequence built inside an email service provider. The sequence sends emails when someone subscribes to a newsletter. The process is set up once, and then continues to operate without any human intervention.

As a writer, you also have manual systems. A daily writing habit is a common example. We cover how to create a writing habit in the next chapter. The purpose of a writing habit is to ensure you make consistent progress on your next book.

Another type of system is a written procedure that you hand off to a virtual assistant or set as a recurring task on your calendar. I have a monthly process during which I update my bookkeeping and review my business metrics. This ensures I never fall behind and am always monitoring my progress.

Notice how all these systems guarantee you follow through with your commitments. You don't want to rely on willpower to get the work done. Research shows that willpower has limits. And while some lucky people may have more willpower than others, we all eventually make the easy choice and skip a difficult assignment.

In a research study published by the National Academy of Sciences, psychologists examined more than 1,100 parole hearing decisions made by U.S. judges. They found that the most influential factor in whether someone was granted parole wasn't their crime, background, or sentences. It was what time of day their case was heard.

"Prisoners who appeared early in the morning received parole about 70% of the time, while those who appeared late in the day were paroled less than 10% of the time."

The study suggests that when judges make repeated rulings, they are more likely to rule in favor of the status quo. In short, you have limited willpower and repeated decisions erode what willpower you have. The answer is to create systems that reduce the amount of decision making and willpower needed to achieve your goals.

There is another reason why systems are important, and that is efficiency. Systems save you time, freeing you to focus on more creative tasks. When an activity is automated, you don't need to expend energy reinventing the wheel. Each time you do the task, you know how to do it.

Having a system also helps you optimize your results. For example, I'm constantly refining my book launch process. When I plan a launch, I map marketing activities to specific days. I then record the number of daily downloads throughout the launch period. This shows me which promotions generate the most book sales. I then use this information to tweak my launch plan for the next title.

As your income as an author grows, you may want to outsource some tasks in your business. This is the final reason why systems are important. As an independent author you're a writer, marketer, publisher, and administrator. Over time, some of these functions can be handed off to other people. If you have already established processes, this transfer runs more smoothly.

Habit Formation

Now, let's discuss the simplest kind of system. When starting out, most of your processes are manual. So, it's helpful to understand how to form habits that stick. At its simplest, a habit has two components: a cue and an action.

The cue is the trigger. It reminds you to perform the habit. For example, a cue could be a calendar notification. You can also chain habits. This is where the cue for a new habit becomes the completion of a habit you have already formed, such as brushing your teeth or pouring your morning coffee.

The action is what you do when cued. It's the essential task you want systematized.

A cue and an action are all you need to form a habit. However, there are ways you can make a habit stickier. For example, you might tag a reward at the end of the action. When you do this your brain knows it's going to be rewarded when you finish and is less likely to resist performing the action.

It also helps to perform your habit in a stable context or an environment. Let's say you're starting a writing habit. You might select a consistent place to associate with the act of writing. Some authors play the same background music when they write, or they have a ritual they perform when they first sit down at their desk.

Something else you will want to do for difficult habits is remove barriers. For the writing habit, this might mean planning what you're going to write in advance. It can also involve starting small. Instead of setting a goal to write 2,000 words a day, you might set a goal to write just 50 words a day.

These are all strategies you can use to speed up the habit-formation process.

System Problems

Before we move on, a cautionary note. Once you automate an activity, it's easy to ignore it. Inefficiencies can creep in. Perhaps a system stops serving you. But because it's happening in the background, you overlook the problem.

While they are powerful, systems can also make you lazy. It's important you don't "set and forget." I recommend reviewing each system on a monthly or quarterly basis. Ask yourself whether it's still creating the desired result. If it isn't, stop or change the system. If it is, look for ways to improve on it. Don't become complacent.

Finally, systems can diminish your personal growth. When you form a habit, you delegate the action to the lower area of your brain. This is separate from the creative part of your brain. I talk more about how to harness the full potential of your brain in section three of this book.

As an author, you want to constantly develop your creative skills. To avoid stagnation, I recommend setting an hour or two aside each day for dedicated focus time. This is when you exercise your higher thinking skills, and this time should be protected at all costs.

In summary, don't seek to over-automate your life. Create routines so that important tasks always get done, but don't take your systems for granted. Leave space for your human qualities, too; they are a vital part of your creative growth.

Action Steps

1. Brainstorm a list of essential tasks you do as an author. Consider these three areas of your business:

Writing: This includes planning, writing, and revising your manuscripts.

Publishing: This involves how you get your books into stores. It can include formatting, editing, cover design, and uploading to publishing platforms.

Promotion: These are activities you do to launch a new book, plus any ongoing marketing to ensure your books keep selling.

In the next three chapters, I describe how to create systems in each of these areas, so you can supercharge your productivity and grow your writing business.

8

WRITE QUICKLY AND EASILY

Even when you think you've mastered the three habits, you will encounter obstacles, like I did while writing this book. I had set myself a timeline of three weeks to complete the first draft. I knew what I wanted to write, and I had a detailed outline. I was ready to go.

I started out strong. I wrote consistently for three days. In fact, my output exceeded any writing I had done before. I was finishing two to three chapters each day. Then on day four, I woke up to a shelter-in-place order. The world was fighting the Coronavirus pandemic. My husband and kids were now at home with me.

It felt like my comfortable existence had been turned on its head. I became confused and unfocused. Suddenly my work seemed unimportant, and so I stopped writing.

The first day I skipped, I told myself I was too busy. I needed to figure out how to homeschool my kids, stock up on groceries, and more. The next day, I felt too distracted to write. The media was filled with Coronavirus news. Friends and family were calling to check in with us. I decided to give myself another day off.

The third day went by, and I still didn't work. My brain continued to offer up excuses why I shouldn't write. It was very convincing. I felt justified in my continued avoidance of work. But the truth was, I was giving in to circumstances.

The Coronavirus pandemic proved the ultimate test of my writing habit. And it didn't stand up to the unexpected changes in my world. However, I did learn two valuable lessons from the experience.

First, when you fail to stick to a habit, don't judge yourself. Berating yourself only adds to your suffering. It's impossible to create quality work if you're frustrated with yourself. When I was ready to get back to writing, I let go of the skipped days. They were in the past. All I could do was focus on how I wanted to move forward.

Second, don't expend energy arguing with reality. Instead focus on your internal state which you can control. In my case, there was no point wishing the virus had never happened or complaining about the situation. What was much more empowering was recognizing that I still had control over my own thoughts and actions.

On the fourth day, I re-established my writing habit. I decided to write early in the morning so that I could spend more time with my family later in the day. I created a quiet place and time where I could focus on finishing this book.

Even during a global pandemic, I was able to get back on track and keep working toward my extraordinary goal. Not because I am special, but because I understand the necessity of making my writing a consistent habit.

Writing Habit

In the previous chapter, I described how a habit has a cue and an action. For your writing habit, the cue is the trigger to start writing and the action is to write.

If you don't already have a regular writing habit, I encourage you to set one now. Decide when to write and set a trigger to help you follow through. This might be an appointment on your calendar or an alarm on your phone. I usually start writing as soon as I've made my morning cup of coffee. Refer to chapter seven for more tips on how to form a new habit.

Your writing habit is unique to you. You may need to adjust it occasionally to fit your external circumstances. But you should aim for consistency. A small amount of effort repeated each day creates a large body of work over the long-term.

Remember, the primary goal of a system is to automate an essential task. However, a system can also increase consistency, improve quality, and save time or money. In the remainder of this chapter, I describe three other processes to enhance your writing output.

Outlining

Here's what George R. R. Martin, author of *The Game Of Thrones*, said about outlining:

"I think there are two types of writers, the architects and the gardeners. The architects plan everything ahead of time, like an architect building a house. They know how many rooms are going to be in the house, what kind of roof they're going to have, where the wires are going to run, what kind of plumbing there's going to be. They have the whole thing designed and blueprinted out before they even nail the first board up. The gardeners dig a hole, drop in a seed and water it. They kind of know what seed it is, they know if [they] planted a fantasy seed or mystery seed or whatever. But as the plant comes up and they water it, they don't know how many branches it's going to have, they find out as it grows. And I'm much more a gardener than an architect."

I'm not going to argue with such a successful author. If you're a gardener and not an architect, then you probably don't need to outline a book to the extent that I do. However, I believe all authors benefit from some degree of planning. Especially nonfiction authors.

It takes energy to switch back and forth between plotting and writing.

When you separate the planning part of writing from the creative side, you use your brain more efficiently. And when you're writing a nonfiction book, it's essential to map out your reader's experience.

A great outline takes your readers on a journey, from where they are now to where they want to be. The final stage in the journey is the resolution of your book's hook. For a nonfiction book, this is usually a solution to a problem or the realization of a dream.

This is the reason why readers buy your book. They want the promised outcome. Deliver on your promise and your readers will love your book. Your outline helps you map out the ideal path so that your readers will experience the transformation they want.

Below is the outlining process I use. You can model your outlining system on mine or devise a distinct method that works for you.

1. Start by brainstorming all your ideas for your book. I use a mind map and do this with pen and paper. Some authors use Post-It notes and write each separate idea on one note.

2. Next, group related ideas together. You can do this by numbering or color-coding ideas on your mind map. If you're using Post-It notes, you can move them around on a big wall or on the floor. Your idea groups are your chapters.

3. Once you have your ideas grouped, put them into a sequence. Think about your reader's journey. What information do they need to learn first? What steps should they take, and in what order, to achieve the promised outcome? You may need to try several outline ideas before you find one that flows.

Notice how brainstorming and organization are discrete steps in the above process. Brainstorming requires the creative part of your brain, whereas organizing uses the planning area. Also, I don't map out every aspect of a book. I leave space for creativity during the writing process. When I write each chapter, I allow new ideas to come to me and incorporate these as appropriate.

Writing Method

We've already discussed your writing habit—when and where you write. Next we look at *how* you write. You may not have spent time thinking about this. Writing may be so natural to you that the idea of breaking it down into a process feels alien. If this is you, stick with me. There is more than one way to write a book. Experimenting with the various options can increase the quality and quantity of your output.

For example, most people type their manuscript on a laptop or PC. But some write longhand on paper. These authors argue that putting pen to paper helps with the creative flow. A 2010 study found that writing by hand stimulates a part of the brain called the Reticular Activating System, the area of the brain associated with learning. I find that when I brainstorm ideas on paper, I come up with more new concepts than I do when typing out my thoughts.

There's a third option. You can also dictate your book. Here's how Kevin J. Anderson, fantasy author, described his dictation process in a podcast interview with Joanna Penn:

I'm a storyteller. I know my novel. I have it all outlined, the hundred chapters or so blocked out with, maybe three or four sentences each. I live in Colorado so I'm in the mountains. It's very beautiful scenery and I'll go out walking with my digital recorder and just tell the story in my head.

*Now, all writers, they think of a sentence and then they type it. Well, I think of the sentence, then I speak it. I'm going through **far fewer steps than somebody who types** it because I can just think it and talk.*

Rather than mentally deconstruct the sentences into words, and then break those words down into letters, and then type those letters on a keyboard so that it comes up on the screen. That's like seven extra steps to type your stuff.

So, I get to go out walking. I can be on a trail somewhere or a smooth bike path and just be away from the telephone, away from the computer, away from the nagging little Facebook icon that wants me to check my Facebook status and Twitter, or whatever. I'm just synced entirely into the story that I'm writing and I usually walk along the trail until I've dictated one chapter. Then I turn around and I have just enough time to dictate another chapter on the way back home.

I email the audio files to a typist who transcribes. Sometimes, I will transcribe it myself if I'm in a real hurry. But I'd rather spend the hour dictating another couple of chapters so that I can move forward.

Notice how Kevin points out that his dictation process requires fewer steps than typing (the emphasis is mine). I've experimented with his system and found this to be true for me too. I average 2,500 words of dictation in one hour, which is double my word count when typing. Also, the process doesn't tire me as much as sitting at a computer and typing. There's a freedom to speaking a book that the creative part of my brain seems to like. Having said that, it takes me longer to revise a dictated piece of writing. And so there are trade-offs.

Your experience may be different. I encourage you to try out different writing methods and be open to finding what works for you. Just because you've written one way for most of your life, it doesn't mean there isn't an alternative that will suit you better.

Revision Process

The final part of the writing process is revising your work. This is where you refine your manuscript before handing it off to a professional editor.

A strict revision process ensures you finish self-editing your manuscript without unnecessary procrastination. It is tempting to keep improving your work. This feels much safer than sharing it with other people. You may tell yourself that if you spend one more week tweaking your manuscript, it will be perfect. However, your book will never be perfect. And this is a wonderful thing. Your book does not need to be flawless to change the lives of your readers.

In my revision process, I review a manuscript three times before sending it to my editor. Here's how it works.

On the first read, look at the big picture and think about your target readers. Here are some questions to ask yourself:

Does the entire book have a logical sequence that takes the reader through a transformation to achieve the end goal?

Does the introduction make a big promise?

Does each chapter flow seamlessly into the next?

Does the concluding chapter leave the reader satisfied?

Does the book inspire the reader to take action?

On the second read, make sure your book is clearly written. This time, you want to read more carefully. Pay attention to how clear and concise your book is.

Is each sentence clear, complete, and concise?

Does each paragraph make one point? Is it clear, complete, and concise?

Does each chapter meet one goal that is part of the entire end goal for the book? Is it clear, complete, and concise? Are there relevant examples or evidence?

Are there any unnecessary words? Some words to be careful of are "really," "very," or just about any adverb.

Are there any duplicate words or phrases that appear near each other? Are there any overused phrases?

Finally, read your book out loud. You want to listen to the rhythm of your book, tweak words to improve readability, and correct any spelling or grammatical errors. Once you complete your final read-through, stop. Don't be tempted to go back and keep changing things.

Action Steps

1. Decide when and where you will write. Make sure you have a strong cue or trigger to remind you to write each day. Then commit to your writing habit.

2. Consider what other systems will enhance your writing. Three discussed in this chapter are outlining, writing method, and revision.

In the next chapter, we talk about publishing processes. Once you've written your book, you want to get it out into the world. I will show you how to use systems to sell more books and grow your income as an author.

9

YOUR PUBLISHING PROCESS

Publishing is the act of preparing and issuing books for sale. It's everything you do between finishing your manuscript and the start of your launch. Publishing isn't always the most exciting part of running a writing business. There are a lot of moving parts to manage. However, how you publish does have a direct impact on your book sales.

Consider another product: Girl Scout Cookies. Where I live, February is Girl Scout Cookie season. Our community is filled with eager Girl Scouts selling their goods. And it would be an underestimation to say that competition is hot.

Each Girl Scout must determine where and when she will sell her cookies. Will she stand outside the local grocery store? Will she ask the parents at school pickup? Will she go door to door in her local neighborhood? She also decides how to present her cookies. Maybe she makes signs or uses a decorated cart to transport the cookies and display them to potential buyers.

I remember reading a story of one enterprising Girl Scout who sold her cookies outside a marijuana dispensary in San Diego. The patrons of the shop were drawn to the sugary treats. The Girl Scout sold 300 boxes in just six hours.

Regardless of what you may think of the ethics of her strategy, it certainly helped increase her sales. Your publishing process does the same for you. It directly impacts how many books you sell and how much money you earn.

Publishing Decisions

Before you define your publishing processes, there are some decisions you need to make. For an independent author, the first decision is whether to sell exclusively on Amazon or publish wide across multiple platforms. I discussed the pros and cons of each option in chapter four.

A second decision involves which formats to publish in, such as eBook, paperback, audiobook, hardback, and large print. You also need to consider your publishing timeline. Are you going to publish on all platforms and in all formats simultaneously? This can be a complex undertaking for an independent author who is doing all the work on their own.

If you're a newer author, I recommend you keep things simple to start with. If there's a market for your book, you can always expand your publishing processes later.

For my first five books, I initially published an eBook on Amazon. I later added paperback and audiobook. I stayed exclusive to Amazon because this allowed me to focus my limited resources in the marketplace with the biggest reach.

I am now publishing my books wide and exploring other options such as foreign translations. However, at the time of this writing, most of my royalties originate from Amazon. Here's the approximate split across the various formats and outlets:

Amazon eBook 45%

Amazon paperback 45%

Audible audiobook 5%

Other non-Amazon platforms 5%

Your split will be different based on many factors, including genre and where you focus your efforts.

Document Your Process

Once you determine formats, retailers, and timeline, you're ready to publish your book. Learning how to publish takes time. There're technologies to learn and many small decisions to make. Recording how you complete each step will save time when you publish future books. You don't want to keep reinventing the wheel. Re-learning the process each time you publish can become tedious.

Documenting your process also ensures consistency. This is important if you have a book series. Having a defined process ensures you deliver the same experience across all books in a series. This includes creating uniform covers, internal layout, front and back matter, and more.

Finally, capturing every step in your publishing process eliminates inefficiencies. When I documented my formatting process, I noticed that I was repeating steps each time I prepared a manuscript for a new platform. Redundancy had crept in when I expanded my distribution outside of Amazon. This led me to design a more streamlined formatting process. Thus, saving time and reducing the likelihood of errors.

You may resist documenting your process. But it doesn't have to be difficult or time-consuming. Next time you publish a book, write out the steps as you do them. Be careful to capture the details. Imagine you're handing the process over to someone else (which you may want to do in the future). What would they need to know in order to execute the system on their own?

If you're struggling to write down your processes, you can also try recording yourself performing each task. The important lesson is to capture everything you do so that next time you—or someone else—can quickly create the same result.

Publishing Steps

Below I have listed the main steps in the publishing process. I describe each of these in detail in my book, *Author Success Blueprint*. You can use this list to organize your publishing documentation. Create a record for each of the steps listed below and for any other tasks that are part of your process.

Book Formatting

Your book's formatting determines the interior layout. You need to prepare your book for every format and platform you publish to. You can either pay a professional to format your book or learn how to do this yourself.

Book Cover

Your book cover must capture the attention of casual browsers. As with formatting, you need a book cover for each format you decide to publish in. If you're not a professional designer, I recommend hiring a professional to create your cover(s) for you.

Book Description

This is the blurb that appears on the back of your book and in the online store. Shoppers read your book description before deciding whether or not to buy. The goal of your description is to show your ideal readers why they must read your book.

Category and Keyword Selection

Categories and keywords help readers discover your book in online stores. They are the equivalent of picking which shelf your book is displayed on at a physical retailer. You don't want to place a business book in the cooking section.

Upload To Publishing Platforms

This is everything you do to upload your manuscript, cover, and meta data (description, keywords, categories) to the various publishing platforms. For example, if you're publishing exclusively to Amazon, then you set up the eBook and paperback in Amazon's Kindle Direct Publishing platform.

There are many tasks involved in publishing a book. Recording your process now saves you time and headaches in the future. To help you get started, you can download my process list and publishing timeline from the bonus area at: sallyannmiller.com/publish.

Action Steps

1. Decide which platforms you want to publish on, the formats, and your overall publishing timeline.

2. Create a document and start capturing the steps in your publishing process.

We're nearly done with systems! In the final chapter in this section, we discuss book promotion. Get ready to streamline your marketing efforts and start selling a lot more books.

10

SELL MORE BOOKS

In the previous chapters, we explored your writing and publishing processes. How you write and publish your book directly impacts your sale numbers. For example, a strong title, cover, and description all contribute to your title's appeal. They tell shoppers why they would want to buy your book.

However, you can't sell a product if nobody knows it exists. Your marketing systems are an essential part of your success as an author. Your objective when promoting is to do one or more of the following:

- Increase awareness: Introduce new people to your product.
- Create interest: Show potential readers how your book meets their needs or desires.
- Generate sales: Directly ask people to buy your book.
- Create reader loyalty: Engage existing readers so they might buy future products.

In this chapter, I provide an overview of the most popular marketing systems that are proven to work for authors. There are thousands of ways you can sell your books. Don't limit yourself to the ones you find here. The main takeaway from this chapter is to pick a few that work for you and then create systems to keep selling your books.

Your job as an author isn't done once you publish. You must be proactive in marketing your title(s). However, this doesn't have to be complex or even time-consuming. If you automate your marketing processes, then you can earn passive income—or nearly passive—for many years to come.

Launch Versus Ongoing Promotion

It's helpful to break down your promotional activities into two distinct phases. What you do at launch and what you do on an ongoing basis.

Your book launch takes place in the first few weeks after a new title is brought to market. Your goal at launch is to garner as much attention as possible for your book. The more sales you get in the first few days, the higher your book will appear in the bestseller lists. A book that ranks high benefits from extra visibility and even gets a helping hand from retailer platforms like Amazon.

Launch tends to be intense and many of the activities are manual. Your focus should be telling people about your new book. You will want to pursue multiple marketing activities in order to reach a wide range of readers. This level of activity is not sustainable over the long-term. Therefore, your ongoing book promotion is lower key. But it's just as important.

After initial launch, your sales numbers will drop. Fiction authors often report a steep decline after the first three months. Nonfiction authors may be able to sustain sales for longer and with less promotion. But there is still a tailing off. The goal of your ongoing promotion is to keep your book selling after the initial flurry dies down.

Launch Promotion Systems

In *Author Success Blueprint*, I describe my entire launch system. The following is an overview of the process I recommend for authors who have between zero and 5,000 followers. This system is designed to maximize your sales by drawing on book promotion sites. More established authors may not need to rely or a free or 99 cent promotion because they can leverage their existing reader base.

During the week before official launch day, your book is in stealth mode. It's live in Amazon's store (and other retailers if you're publishing wide) but you're not actively promoting it. During this week, check to ensure everything is uploaded correctly to Amazon. Also, email your advance readers and request reviews. Book reviews are an important part of your launch system. Reviews tell shoppers and Amazon that your book is popular.

On launch day, make sure your book is either free or priced at 99 cents. Then start telling the world about your book. Email your followers, spread the word about your book via social media and in any relevant online communities. Emphasize that your book is discounted for a short time only.

Also leverage book promotion sites during your launch period. A promotion site builds a list of people who enjoy book deals. For a fee, typically between $5 and $100, they share your book with their followers. If you do not have a large audience, submitting your book to promotion sites is the fastest way to reach thousands of readers.

After a week or so, increase your book price. The exact timing depends on your promotions and how well your book is doing in the paid charts. The optimal time to increase your price is when your book is still climbing the rankings.

As you can see from the above summary, there are many moving parts to a launch. It's easy to drop the ball and forget to do something. As with your publishing process, I recommend documenting your launch system. List all the activities you do during a launch and on which days. You can download my launch timeline from the bonus area here: sallyannmiller.com/publish.

Documenting your launch process saves you time and stress in subsequent launches. It also means you can analyze your book's performance and look for ways to improve next time.

For example, I track the number of downloads over the first seven days of a launch. I then map the exact promotional activities I perform on each day. This gives me a picture of which actions generate the most sales, so that in my next launch, I can put more resources into the promotions that have the greatest impact.

Ongoing Promotion Systems

The goal of your ongoing promotion is to maintain book sales. If you do nothing after launch, your sales eventually dwindle to a handful each month. However, with a relatively small amount of effort, you can keep generating revenue each week. The key is to identify which activities work best for you and the type of books you write. Then automate these actions as much as possible.

Below is a list of suggested strategies. Do not attempt to implement all of these. There's no one marketing strategy that guarantees your success. All the following methods take time before gaining traction. And some work better for different audiences. As always, the key is to find the approach that works for you. Pick one or two strategies and give them your full attention for several months. If you're not seeing an increase in sales, then tweak your approach or move on to the next. Know yourself and discover what works best for you.

Finally, make sure your overall ongoing marketing achieves all four of the following objectives:

- Increase awareness.
- Create interest.
- Generate sales.
- Create reader loyalty.

Author Website

If you're building a writing business, then you need a website. This is your home base. It's where you direct people who want to find out more about you and your books.

Your author website can also help you connect with new readers. To do this, you need to implement search engine optimization (SEO). An SEO strategy helps people find your author site by telling Google (and other search engines) what your website is about. However, it's worth noting that the Internet is fairly saturated, so SEO is less effective than it was ten years ago.

Your author website can help:

- Increase awareness: People can find you by searching on the Internet.
- Create interest: Show potential readers what kinds of books you write.
- Generate sales: Directly ask people to buy your book.
- Create reader loyalty: Engage existing readers by publishing content on a blog, podcast, or video platform.

Social Media

Many authors leverage the power of social media to build a large audience. However, be careful about spending too much time on social media. A large social media following doesn't always translate into more book sales and a bigger income.

Research the different social media platforms to see where your potential readers are hanging out, then pick a platform and dive in. No matter which platform you decide to use, here are some tips to help you promote your content.

1. Experiment with the style of your posts to see what type of content your followers engage with.

2. Use your data. See which posts are performing (e.g. by sending

readers to your website or sales pages) and look for patterns. Find out when your users are active and adjust your posting schedule accordingly.

3. Use scheduling tools to help you schedule posts in bulk. This way you aren't glued to social media all day long.

4. Remember to build relationships. Respond to comments and join the conversation on other people's posts when you can.

Social media can help:

- Increase awareness: new readers find you organically.
- Create interest: show potential readers what kinds of books you write.
- Generate sales: directly ask people to buy your book.
- Create reader loyalty: engage existing readers by posting on social media.

Other People's Audiences

When you connect with influencers in your space, you can share your books with someone else's audience. One way to do this is by guest posting. This is when you write a post that someone else publishes on their blog.

You often receive a bio at the end of your guest post and can include a link back to your blog. This way, readers who are interested can click through and find you. It also gives you an external link to your blog, which is beneficial.

Guest posting isn't the only way to leverage someone else's audience. Being interviewed on a podcast or on a YouTube channel is a quick and easy way to connect with new people.

Other people's audiences can help:

- Increase awareness: reach new readers.

- Create interest: show potential readers what kinds of books you write.

Collaboration

As you make connections in your niche and with other authors, you discover opportunities to collaborate. There are many ways to collaborate. For example, you can do a newsletter swap. This is where two authors promote each other's book to their email subscribers. It's a popular strategy with fiction authors who write in the same genre, such as sweet romance.

You can also take part in an online summit, organize a joint webinar, or write a round-up post in which you link to other authors' content and then ask them to share your post.

The key to a successful collaboration is to build relationships with people who have an audience like yours and who share your values. Then work together in a way that benefits everyone.

Collaboration can help:

- Increase awareness: reach new readers via someone else's audience.
- Create interest: show potential readers what kinds of books you write.
- Generate sales: directly ask people to buy your book.

Paid Advertising

This next marketing strategy is not recommended for beginners. You only want to pay for advertising once you know people buy your book and have a clear picture of who your ideal readers are. If you start doing paid advertising too early, you risk spending thousands of dollars targeting the wrong people and getting zero return on your investment.

Facebook and Amazon advertising are popular forms of paid advertising for authors. Other options include BookBub advertising, Pinterest advertising, Google AdWords, and YouTube advertising.

In all cases, you must be clear on who you are targeting, what those people want, and how you are going to get a return on your ad expenditure.

Paid advertising can help:

- Increase awareness: new readers find you.
- Create interest: show potential readers what kinds of books you write.
- Generate sales: directly ask people to buy your book.
- Create reader loyalty: engage existing readers who may be missing your content, for example, by targeting them on Facebook.

Email Marketing

As with your website, email marketing is essential for any author who is serious about growing their business. Email marketing is less about building a following and more about forming a relationship with readers who have already discovered your books.

Most experts agree that your email list is more important than your social media following. Social media networks are always changing their algorithms. The people who follow you might not see the content you share. You don't own the platforms, and you don't have any say in changes that happen.

What you do own, however, is your email list. It's your direct line to your readers. Before you can start collecting email addresses, you need to sign up for an email service provider like ConvertKit or MailerLite. You can then add signup forms to your website and inside your books so that your readers can enter their email address and join your list.

Email marketing can help:

- Generate sales: directly ask people to buy your book.
- Create reader loyalty: engage existing readers by sending a regular newsletter.

Action Steps

1. Document your book launch process. You can download mine as a starting point here: sallyannmiller.com/publish

2. Select two or more ongoing marketing strategies and commit to these for the next three months. At a minimum, make sure you're building an email list.

As you work through these action steps, take time to familiarize yourself with how successful authors in your field sell their books. Study their websites and follow the authors who interest you. What marketing strategies are they using? Learn from the people who are already doing what you want to do. This is how you create your own successful writing business and start making a difference in the world.

SECTION THREE
HABIT THREE: BELIEVE IN YOURSELF

11

TAKE CHARGE OF YOUR LIFE

We all love a good underdog story. David versus Goliath. Buster Douglas versus Mike Tyson. Erin Brockovich versus PG&E. When I read these stories or watch these events, I always want to know one thing. Why does the underdog emerge victorious?

The answer lies in habit three. The victor has self-belief, whereas the loser does not. When I watch a sporting upset, I can always spot the moment the losing team stops believing. This is the instant self-doubt sets in and their performance suffers. Even successful people are prone to a sudden loss of confidence.

If you want to reach your full potential as an author, you must become proficient in the third habit and practice it constantly. Here's what habit three tells us:

Successful authors accept responsibility for their results and believe in their power to achieve the desired outcome, no matter what happens.

Habit three is all about adopting the right mindset. Everyone has a set of ingrained beliefs. You tell yourself stories about the situation you're in. Some of your beliefs hold you back. It may be your ideas about money—how much you deserve, your ability to earn, your spending or saving habits. Or it may be your beliefs about what you're capable of or what others think about you.

Habit three is something you will work on forever. But it's essential you do so. The greatest difference between the six-figure author and the writer who is scraping by is their level of self-belief.

Your Thoughts

We start by examining how your thoughts influence your results. This will help you see that you already have the power to take charge of your life.

Imagine you're writing your next title and your main thought is, "My work isn't good enough."

This thought leads to discouragement. You work on your book from a place of self-doubt. Your words lack conviction. You fail to connect with your reader at the deepest possible level.

Let's say you finish your book and you push forward, but you still have the thought, "My work isn't good enough." When you publish, you avoid telling people about your new book, or you do it in a tentative way. People sense your doubt and they don't buy your book.

Now, imagine you had a different thought. Perhaps you thought, instead, "This book will change my readers' lives."

You feel inspired when you write. You're excited to share your ideas with the world. You pour everything you have into your book and produce your best work. When you publish, you can't wait to tell people about it. Readers feel your enthusiasm and rush to buy your book. Then they tell their friends and sales take off.

In both these fictional scenarios, you're the same person. You have identical skills and ideas. The only difference is in your thinking. Fearful thoughts create mediocre results. Positive thoughts lead to equally positive outcomes.

Below are some more thoughts which are poisonous to writers. Don't judge yourself if any of these are familiar. These thoughts are normal. We all have them. Judging your thoughts is just one more way for your brain to make you suffer. Instead, use the following as a guidepost to see where you need to work on your self-belief. I show you how to do this in the next two chapters.

I'm not a good enough writer.

Nobody will buy my book.

Writers don't make much money.

I can't make a living from my writing.

This is too hard.

I don't have enough time to write.

I'm no good with the tech side of publishing.

Marketing will make me look sales-y.

My friends and family will laugh at me.

It takes at least a year to write a good book.

I'll never be as good as [insert your favorite author].

This will never work for me.

So, where do these thoughts come from? Why do you see the negative more quickly than the positive? And why does this seem to happen against your own volition? The answer lies in how your lower brain has evolved.

In today's busy world, it's easy to move through life on autopilot—shifting from one task to the next without pausing to reflect on what you're doing or why. You are too busy. Too caught up in day-to-day life to stop and notice how things are unfolding for you.

In this state, you aren't always conscious of how your brain is operating. You're letting it do its own thing without much supervision. And some parts of your brain have strong ideas about how you should live.

Take the amygdala for example. This tiny structure in your lower brain has evolved to detect threats and tell your body how to respond. From your amygdala's perspective, you're surrounded by physical and emotional danger. Your amygdala thinks unfamiliar situations could result in rejection by the tribe, or even death.

It works hard to keep you safely within your comfort zone. Your lower brain can have you reacting before you've even noticed what you're doing or why you're doing it. This can be handy if, for example, you're about to be hit by a car and need to move quickly to get out of the way.

But your amygdala can view all new activities as life-threatening, including writing a book or starting a business. If you let your amygdala and other parts of your lower brain run the show, then you'll spend your days on the sofa, eating chocolate and binge-watching Downton Abbey.

The antidote is to practice habit three. You start by observing your thoughts and feelings, and then learn to act on purpose regardless of the thoughts your lower brain serves you. Fortunately, there are other parts of your brain that can help you do this. In the upcoming chapters, I show you how to harness the power of your higher brain to build your self-belief.

Stages of Self-Belief

When you have self-belief, you accept yourself fully. You do not need external validation. And you don't judge or shame yourself. You know you are already enough, and nothing can change that. There's not a single thing you or anyone else can say, think, or do that can reduce your worthiness.

You are also willing to experience any emotion and act in the face of fear. This is what makes habit three so powerful. When you believe in yourself, anything is possible.

And yet full self-belief is unattainable for most people. Almost all humans, deep down, doubt their worthiness. Hidden in your thoughts is a belief that there's something wrong with you. This is the ultimate source of human suffering.

Before we go any further, I'd like to offer you an alternative possibility. Maybe—just maybe—you are one hundred percent worthy.

I'll be honest here. This idea is something I grasp intellectually, but I struggle to believe it all the time. And so, I understand if you find this concept challenging. You'll work on habit three for the rest of your life. Few people believe in themselves all the time. However, with practice, you can move the needle in the right direction.

In the rest of this book, you will learn how to generate self-belief. It won't be easy. Having self-belief means accepting your humanness for what it is. It's acting when you're feeling afraid or unsure. Self-belief does not eliminate the fear. Instead, you let yourself feel it all, then go ahead and create anyway.

There are three stages to increasing your self-belief and ultimately your success as an author. They are: awareness, acceptance, and action.

The first stage is awareness. You cannot manage something unless you can see it clearly. You want to gain clarity around your inner state, which is comprised of your thoughts and emotions. Brooke Castillo of The Life Coach School taught me that our thoughts create our feelings. Our feelings drive our actions. And our actions determine our results.

I'll never forget the first time I listened to The Life Coach School podcast. I heard Brooke say this:

"If you want to have a result you've never had before, you have to have a thought you've never thought before."

Hearing this was a light bulb moment for me. I finally understood that my reality is first created in my mind. If I wanted to build more success as an author, I had to change the way I thought. In short, your inner state (thoughts and emotions) determine your outer state (actions and results). Therefore, before you can change your results you must learn to manage your thoughts and emotions.

As a writer, my favorite exercise to increase awareness is journaling. I write about my thoughts and feelings every day, usually in the morning. I also journal when I'm struggling with a problem. This practice helps me step back from my thoughts and observe what's happening inside my brain. I describe how to increase your awareness through journaling in chapter twelve.

Once you're aware of your inner state, the next stage is acceptance. Having negative thoughts and feelings doesn't imply there's something wrong with you. In fact, it means the opposite. You're functioning perfectly as an evolved human being.

Acceptance is knowing your thoughts and feelings are what make you human. They exist and there's no need to judge them. Instead, see them for what they are and don't let them rule your actions.

Accepting your thoughts and feelings means not pushing them away or reacting to them. Rather, you want to allow the emotions to process through your body. I explain how to do this in chapter thirteen. I also show you how to recognize and break your default behavior patterns so you can get out of your own way and create greater success in your writing business.

The final stage of self-belief is taking action from a positive energy. Once you're aware of your patterns and have learned to break them, you can practice taking action regardless. In chapter fourteen, I explain how to tap into powerful thoughts and feelings that will drive you to create superior results in your life.

Action Steps

1. Read the common thoughts listed at the start of this chapter. Write down the ones you recognize. Avoid judging yourself. We all have fears, doubts, and reasons that hold us back. Simply practice becoming aware of what your lower brain tells you.

2. Next, review the personal mission statement you created in chapter three. In a journal, write down all the reasons why following your mission is important to you. Then re-commit to living your purpose.

Now that you understand how your inner state determines your outer results, you are ready to start practicing the three stages of self-belief. In the next chapter, you will discover exactly what's holding you back from creating more success in your career as an author.

12

WATCH YOUR BRAIN

By now, you can see how your lower brain will run your life if left unsupervised. In this chapter, you will practice the first stage of self-belief by becoming aware of what's happening inside your mind. If you're new to watching your thoughts, be patient with yourself. Creating separation between your higher and lower brain is an art. It's something you'll be practicing for the rest of your life.

This work is transformative. There are many resources that teach you writing craft, publishing systems, and marketing strategies. Habit three is different. It's what separates the highly successful authors from those who fail to live up to their potential.

When you commit to practicing habit three, you will:

- Believe beyond your current results.
- Set bigger and more exciting goals.
- Take more action and more risks.
- Achieve more in your writing business.
- Live into your purpose.

Sound good? Let's start by learning to watch your thoughts and feelings.

Journaling Exercise

Journaling is a powerful way to build awareness of your inner state. The practice is simple. There are three steps:

1. In your journal, write down all the thoughts and feelings you are experiencing. If this seems too overwhelming, start with a topic or question. Then write down all the thoughts relating to the topic or question. A topic might be "family," "money," or "writing."

2. Once you've finished writing, re-read your notes. Separate the facts from the story. Usually, there are few facts. Almost all of what is happening in your brain is invented by your mind. I show you how to do this step in the example below.

3. Finally, question whether the story you're telling yourself is serving you. All thoughts are optional and can be questioned. As we saw in the previous chapter, our inner state creates our results. Where you have negative thoughts, look for reasons why the opposite story might also be true for you. The example below demonstrates how this works.

When you do this exercise, make sure you get everything out of your head. Don't censor yourself. Allow your brain to complain. You want to clearly see the facts of your situation versus your thoughts and feelings.

By way of example, I want to share one of my journal entries. But first, a little background: I'm writing this book in March 2020. The world is currently experiencing a pandemic. External events are moving at a rapid pace. I wrote the following journal entry the day after my children's schools were closed and the state of California (where I live) had been ordered to stay home.

I want to escape my emotions. There's a constant dull feeling in my stomach. It's uncomfortable. When I slow down to observe the feeling it's heavy and angry. Wow—angry. I wasn't expecting that. I thought my predominant feeling was anxiety. So, why am I angry?

I'm angry because my life is upside down. I can't control what's happening. I feel like life is happening to me and it's moving too fast. I'm angry that my kids and husband are home with me. I can't leave the house. And I don't know for how long. I'm angry that my quiet work time has been taken away from me. I just want everything to go back to normal.

But I also feel shame. Because there are others in far worse situations. I'm acting like a child. There's nothing wrong with my life. I should be able to handle these changes.

I wrote a lot more than this. I had many reasons why I was angry. And even more reasons why I should feel ashamed. I share this example because it's easy to see the story I am creating in my head. Also, I want to show you that it's okay to have these kinds of thoughts. This is what we do as humans. Mine is an extreme example—my inner state isn't usually in such turmoil—but it beautifully demonstrates how we create our own suffering.

Here are some of the thoughts from my journaling exercise. None of these are real. They are all inventions of my human mind.

My life is upside down.

Life is happening to me and it's moving too fast.

My quiet work time has been taken away from me.

I want everything to go back to normal.

I'm acting like a child.

I can't leave my house.

There's nothing wrong with my life.

I should be able to handle these changes.

The last thought contains the word "should." Whenever you find yourself using this word in relation to yourself, be alert. This indicates that either shame or guilt is lurking beneath the surface. In my case, the true thought is:

I'm not handling these changes and that makes me a bad person.

Now, let's look at the facts in my journal entry. There's only one:

My kids and husband are in the house with me.

"I can't leave my house" is not a fact. It's a thought that I'm having because my area is under a shelter-in-place order. It's a somewhat dramatic thought, too! I can leave the house to exercise outdoors, to buy groceries, or to visit the doctor.

Separating story from facts gives you space. You gain perspective over your life. You can see how your brain is creating your reality. Once you can see this, you have the power to question your thoughts and create a new reality if you so desire.

However, you don't want to rush into new thoughts. There's a step you must take first. This is especially important when you notice shame or self-judgment in your thoughts. Stage two of self-belief is acceptance. You must allow your human emotions without judgment.

The Self-Judgment Trap

When you practice awareness, you may be tempted to judge your thoughts. It can be difficult to look at the inner workings of your mind. Please know that any thoughts you're having are normal. It's essential to avoid falling into the self-judgment trap.

Self-criticism is the fastest way to compound a negative emotion. You add suffering to a painful thought by shaming yourself. This is a common pattern and you must be vigilant if you want to sidestep it. Here are some examples of the self-judgment trap:

You're angry with your toddler and shout at him. Then you feel bad about shouting at your child.

You're stressed and drop your mother's favorite vase on the floor. Then you beat yourself up for being so clumsy.

You're feeling awkward in a social situation and blurt out something inappropriate. Then you judge yourself for saying something foolish.

You feel nervous about presenting an idea in a work meeting and stumble over your words. Afterward, you tell yourself that you ruined the meeting.

In each of these common scenarios, you take a negative emotion and make it worse with self-judgment. You're feeling bad and intensify the negativity by judging yourself. Before you increase your self-belief, you need to recognize and avoid this cycle.

The antidote to self-judgment is understanding. And the path to understanding is through compassion or curiosity.

Ultimately, you want to develop self-compassion. Inner confidence comes from accepting yourself. This means loving yourself, even the parts you want to hide from the outside world. Self-compassion means accepting the truth of what it means to be human.

Many people struggle to treat themselves kindly. Your brain is wired to look for the negative. You automatically believe the thoughts your brain serves you. The self-judgment trap feels familiar, even comfortable, despite the increased suffering it causes.

If self-compassion feels out of reach, then try being curious. Be interested in how your brain is working and why. Seek to understand the thoughts you are having. You can use the journaling exercise described earlier in this chapter to examine your thoughts. Question what's true and what's a story.

Through careful inquiry, you will begin to see that your thoughts are not fact, and yet they create the reality you live in. You can then decide whether to keep thoughts that cause you pain or whether to let them go.

Deeper Inquiry

Before we close this chapter, I want to share one more exercise that can help develop your awareness. I learned this from Tara Brach, psychologist and mindfulness teacher.

When you're journaling about your thoughts, ask yourself this question:

What really wants my attention?

Then, ask the follow up question:

What don't I want to feel right now?

You have tens of thousands of thoughts each day. Often the first thought or emotion you identify is a reaction to another deeper feeling. One that you don't want to experience.

When I reviewed my journal entry on the first day of the pandemic, I knew that beneath my anger there was another emotion which I was avoiding. Anger is a reactive feeling. One that we gravitate toward in response to something we don't like or don't want to acknowledge.

Later the same day, I sat down in a quiet space, silenced my mind, and asked myself this question: "What really wants my attention?"

The answer came to me immediately. Anxiety.

Beneath the anger, I was afraid. I felt anxious about the future. Intellectually, I knew the pandemic would end. But in the moment, my fear around current events was pervasive. With this knowledge, I was able to have compassion for myself and all the other people who were feeling the same as I was. Eventually, I felt able to move on to the second and third stages of self-belief. I processed my negative emotions, then tapped into a different energy so I could finish writing this book.

Now, it's your turn to practice awareness. In the action steps, I provide an exercise to help you observe your inner world. I encourage you to bring curiosity and compassion to this process. Seek to understand your inner state without judgment.

Action Steps

1. Find a quiet place and write down your answers to this question: "What am I thinking and feeling right now?"

2. Review your answer to question one and separate the thoughts from the facts. Avoid the temptation to judge your thoughts. Simply notice how the facts are few and your reality is being created by your inner state.

3. Next, go deeper. Ask yourself this question: "What really wants my attention?" The purpose of this question is to listen to the deepest most vulnerable part of you. Also, ask yourself, "What don't I want to feel right now?"

4. Choose to let go of any self-judgment and resistance. In the next chapter, I share more tools to help you do this. You will learn how to experience your negative emotions and become fearless in your writing career.

13

BECOMING FEARLESS

Once you are aware of your inner state, the second stage of self-belief is acceptance. In the previous chapter, you learned how to watch your thoughts and feelings without judgment. Understanding how your brain operates is the gateway to self-belief. Next, you must walk through the opening and learn how to embrace your emotions—both the good and the bad.

Complete acceptance means being willing to process any emotion through your body. I realize not everyone likes talking about feelings, but trust me here. Managing your emotions is key to mastering habit three and furthering your success as an author.

When you're willing to experience any feeling, there's nothing you can't do. This is the secret to fulfilling your potential and creating a breakthrough in your business and life.

What Are Emotions?

If you think about an emotion and take the experience of it, not the thoughts you have, but the affect in your body, what does it feel like?

For example, consider fear, which most often holds us back in our writing careers—especially the fear of failure or rejection. Most people don't want to risk being wrong. This is normal.

Our human brains have evolved to protect us from rejection. For our ancestors, being cast out from the tribe meant certain death. They needed other humans to help with gathering food, taking care of the young, and building a shelter. Today, the fear of rejection is less useful. Being excluded doesn't mean death. Plus, the fear keeps you stuck. It prevents you from showing up and doing your best work.

When you think about rejection or humiliation as an experience, what arises inside your body?

Perhaps you redden and feel your skin covered in heat. Maybe there's a sinking feeling in your stomach. The sensations might be small or big in intensity.

The physical experience of a negative emotion isn't that big of a deal. It only becomes worse when your thoughts engage with the emotion. When you judge yourself or your situation. When you dwell on what's happening and create new reasons in your mind to feel bad.

It's your thinking that makes the experience difficult to bear.

The key to achieving more in your writing career is to accept your emotions without creating additional suffering in your mind.

Default Patterns

Before we talk about how to process your emotions, it's helpful to explore your brain's default behavior. There are three ways most people respond when they experience discomfort. They either react, resist, or reduce the emotion.

Let's explore these in more detail so that you can become aware of your default patterns. These are the automatic behaviors that stand between you and success as an author.

When faced with a new situation, your brain works to stop you from experiencing painful emotions. It's determined to prevent you from risking rejection, humiliation, or failure. If you want to grow as a writer, you must override this lifetime of default programming.

Reacting to Emotions

Imagine you're about to publish a book. Doing so means allowing other people to form an opinion about you and your work. Your brain sees this as a threatening situation. What if someone hates you or your book? What if nobody buys it? What if people don't take you seriously?

These thoughts create fear or self-doubt. You don't want to experience any of these outcomes because you're scared about how they will make you feel. So, you avoid publishing your book. You delay launching or you launch quietly. Perhaps you even give up on your dreams altogether.

These are all ways of reacting to negative emotions.

Another way you might react is with anger or frustration. When events don't go as you want, you feel bad and want to escape that feeling. You might lash out at people around you or start blaming external circumstances for what's happened.

Self-judgment is another form of reaction. We discussed the dangers of self-judgment in the previous trap. Reacting to bad feelings is a normal human response, but it never creates the results you want in your life.

Resisting Emotions

The second way you might respond to discomfort is by resisting it. A good way to explain resistance is with an analogy.

My kids like to play a pool game where they stand on a large, inflatable ball. They push it down beneath the water and balance on top. Of course, the inflatable always slips out from under them and pops up to the surface again.

The same happens when you resist emotions. If you push down—or resist—an emotion, it always reappears. Often, it comes back bigger than before. In the meantime, you've expended unnecessary energy trying to fight the feeling.

This looks like gritting your teeth and using willpower to fight your way through a difficult situation. You're not experiencing the fear. Instead, you are pushing the feelings and thoughts away. This may work in the short-term but it ultimately leads to increased stress, burnout, and poor-quality work.

When you're resisting, you're replacing one bad feeling with another. For example, you might replace fear with desperation. You are acting from a negative action energy. And this never creates positive results.

Reducing Emotions

The final default behavior is numbing yourself to reduce or eliminate the feeling. This is where you indulge in an activity to "take the edge off," or avoid the emotion altogether. Some people numb with food, alcohol, social media, shopping, or Netflix. The list of tricks your brain plays on you is endless.

Sometimes learning can be a way of reducing fear. If you are constantly learning without acting on what you've learned, then chances are you're studying to avoid uncertainty.

Here's another example: Have you ever found yourself mindlessly flicking through your social media feed, but you don't remember picking up your phone? Your brain has learned that social media—or any other favorite distraction—gives you a pleasant dopamine hit. It tricks you into chasing the short-term buzz to escape the negative feelings.

If you recognize any of these behaviors in yourself, then that's good news! You're becoming aware of your default patterns. Please don't judge yourself; all these ways of handling fear are natural human responses. They mean you have an evolved human brain that wants to keep you safe.

Processing Emotions

Now that you know the three ways you don't want to handle your negative emotions, what should you do instead?

The answer is to practice allowing your emotions. This is a tricky concept to teach. The best way to learn is to practice it. Over and over again. Here is what allowing an emotion looks like.

When you notice you want to avoid a negative feeling, stop what you're doing. If you've already started to react, resist, or reduce then pause. Notice how the emotion feels in your body. Try labeling it. Is it fear, stress, anxiety, or overwhelm? Describe the physical sensations. Where in your body do you feel it? Is it hot or cold? What color is it? Is it hard or soft?

Avoid indulging in your thoughts about the feeling. Instead, open to the experience of it. Process the fear through your body. The physical emotion is never as bad as the thoughts you have about it.

It can help to meditate or breathe into the emotion, be willing to let it be there and don't be in a rush for it to go away. If you notice yourself reacting to or resisting the emotion, bring yourself back to the present.

If the emotion becomes too intense, you can also try observing it. This is a subtle skill that's similar to watching your thoughts. But instead you are witnessing yourself feel an emotion. Your body is experiencing the sensation, while the higher part of your brain watches it happen. I find this creates relief while also allowing the emotion to be present.

When you shift into watcher mode, you're able to stay with difficult emotions for longer. You don't feel overwhelmed by the physical experience. As you develop this skill, you are no longer afraid of feeling your own emotions. You can process them instead of storing negative energy in your body. And best of all, you are willing to do anything—no matter what emotion comes up.

Action Steps

Think about a situation or activity in your writing business that brings up strong negative emotions such as fear, uncertainty, humiliation, self-doubt, frustration, or confusion.

1. Answer the following questions about the situation or activity:

What is the situation? Describe it in two or three sentences.

How do you feel about the situation? Name the negative emotion(s).

What is it that makes you feel this way?

2. Now, write about what you do and don't do when you feel the negative emotion(s). Can you identify any patterns such as reacting, resisting, or reducing the emotions?

3. Set aside time each day to check in with the physical sensations in your body and practice processing your emotions. As you become more skilled at doing this, practice allowing negative feelings like fear, anxiety, and overwhelm.

We have explored the first two stages of habit three. You have practiced awareness and are learning to process your emotions. In the final chapter, we dive into stage three of building self-belief. You will discover how to maximize your success as an author by taking positive action.

14

POSITIVE ACTION

If you've stuck with me and completed all the action steps in this section, congratulations. Practicing habit three is challenging work. It can also be revealing. It's like peeling back the layers of an onion. Each time you make one self-discovery, you realize there are more layers beneath it.

I encourage you to be gentle with yourself. And remember—no self-judgment! Don't add to a negative state by judging your thoughts and feelings.

If you find yourself resisting this work, I ask you to keep an open mind. When I first discovered mindfulness techniques, I also had doubts. My practical side rejected the idea. It felt intangible and I mentally labeled it as "positive thinking nonsense."

Yet, as I deepened my study, the same ideas kept popping up in unlikely places. Not just in spiritual teachings, but also in the fields of psychology, philosophy, quantum physics, and neuroscience. As I applied the concepts to my life, I began to see shifts in different areas. My health, relationships, career, and personal well-being all improved.

When you commit to habit three, you remove the limits you have subconsciously placed on yourself. In this final chapter, I show you how to create as an author in a much more powerful way. You will learn how to harness positive action energy to grow your writing career. This is the final stage to growing your self-belief and mastering habit three.

Goals and Suffering

Before we explore positive action, you need to understand why most authors struggle. The problem starts with goal setting. There's nothing wrong with goals (more on that below). But there is an issue when the goal becomes your reason for being.

Having a goal often leads to a sense of striving. You become attached to the desired outcome. You want the result more than you want to do the work to get there. This "wanting" colors everything you do. It ruins your experience and the quality of your work.

Instead of enjoying the process of growing your career, you focus on the future. You yearn for how you think you'll feel when you finally reach your goal. This is a fruitless exercise, since achieving your goal won't help you feel any better in the long-term.

Think about the last time you set a goal and achieved it. How did you feel at your moment of victory? Perhaps you had a brief buzz of excitement, but the feeling soon passed, and you found yourself looking for an even bigger goal to work toward.

Attachment to goals is the source of your struggle. Don't misunderstand me here. I still believe in goals. I showed you how to set effective goals in chapter five. However, even with a meaningful goal, it's easy to cling to some imagined future, one that you believe is better than your current situation. When you do this, you're acting from a closed and restricted place. This puts limitations on what you can create in the world.

The conflict between goals and living in the present is something I've long wrestled with. The resolution I've found most helpful lies in understanding the emotion or energy you are acting from.

Action Energy

In previous chapters we examined how negative emotions create undesirable results. It can be helpful to think about the emotion driving your action as a type of energy.

In science, energy is the power behind sources such as electricity and coal which make machines or systems work. Some energy sources are more efficient than others. The most efficient are renewable sources, like wind and sunlight. These are natural resources that are not finite or exhaustible.

Now, if we take this concept and apply it to the energy driving our human actions, then we want to use the most efficient or easily renewable energy source. Imagine having unlimited energy to create and sell more books in your writing business. That's exactly what happens when you work from positive action energy.

The problem is most people are acting from negative action energy. This type of energy is quickly expended, and slow to renew. Imagine you're working in your writing business and you are focused on external results: how many readers you have, how much money you're making, or how many influencers you know. This is understandable; it's how most people operate. We live in a culture of wanting more. More money, more recognition, a bigger house, another car. Your brain's default setting is desire.

However, this wanting keeps you stuck on a treadmill because "more" is never enough. As soon as your brain receives one reward, it casts around for the next. The wanting never stops.

So, how do you get off the treadmill? The solution is not to pursue a different goal. It's to change the emotion or energy you're acting from. You need to switch from a negative action energy to a positive action energy.

When you're operating from negative action energy, you're attached to the outcome. Life feels like a struggle and you tire easily. Below are some negative action feelings. This isn't a proscriptive list. Your negative emotions may be different. Some of these feelings may even be positive for you.

Needy

Clingy

Grasping

Competitive

Envious

Convincing (especially when selling something)

Justified

Entitled

Eager

Determined

Notice how the last two seem like positive emotions. And perhaps they are for you. We all respond differently to the range of human feelings. Eagerness and determination are negative experiences for me, because when I feel them there's a tightness in my body. My thoughts center around wanting a result. I find little to no satisfaction in either the process or the outcome.

The physical tightness and the attachment thoughts are all key indicators that you're in negative action energy. Negative emotions feel closed and constricted. In contrast, positive action energy feels open and expansive. There is no attachment. You feel more alive. You are living fully in the present. You are open to possibility.

Positive energy constantly renews itself, whereas negative energy leaves you drained.

Creative people often describe the experience of positive action energy as following their muse or being in a state of flow. When you act from positive energy, your experience and results are more satisfying. You enjoy the journey and create from a higher place.

Below are some positive energy feelings. Again, your list may look different from mine. The key is to notice how you're feeling when you're fully present in a task.

Accepting

Allowing

Inspired

Engaged

Curious

Enthusiastic

Open

Fascinated

Abundant

The first two emotions—accepting and allowing—are weaker than the others, but I include them because it's not always possible to love everything you do. Sometimes it's enough to accept the necessity of your work, stop resisting and allow the present moment to be as it is. Flowing with life is much easier than fighting it or clutching at the future.

Finding Thoughts

So far, you've practiced being aware of your inner state and you've learned how to experience negative emotions without reacting, resisting, or avoiding them. In this step, we discuss finding new thoughts that create positive action energies that better serve you in growing your success as an author.

Review the extraordinary goal you set in chapter five. Ask yourself what feeling will create this result for you. Review the list of positive energy feelings above and see if any resonate, or think about a difficult goal you achieved in the past. What emotion drove you to create that result? The emotion is different for each person. Experiment to find the feeling that drives you to perform at your highest level.

Think about what you need to believe in order to create this feeling. It must be something you *can* believe at least 50 percent of the time. If you're struggling to come up with a thought, try completing the following sentence: "It's possible that I can [achieve extraordinary goal]." Write the thought in your journal.

Each day, review your new thought. Practice the thought and feeling. Note, this exercise won't banish the negative beliefs you already have. They will still emerge, especially when you face obstacles on your way to creating the desired result. When you experience negative emotions, practice being present with your feelings using the exercise in the previous chapter. Then remind yourself of the new thought and feeling. From this positive place, it is much easier to take the required action to grow your business.

Tolle's Modalities

As I was forming this concept of negative versus positive action energy, I re-read *A New Earth* by Eckhart Tolle. Toward the end of his book, Tolle describes what he calls the three modalities of awakened doing. They are:

Acceptance

Enjoyment

Enthusiasm

When I read about Tolle's modalities, I was struck by their similarity to positive action energy. Tolle argues that when you act from one of these three emotions, the quality of your actions becomes empowered. Whereas, when you act from any other energy, what you do is influenced by your ego, which ultimately creates suffering for yourself and others.

Here's a quick summary of the three modalities.

Acceptance occurs when you can't find joy in a task, but you still do it willingly. You stop resisting the act of doing and are at peace.

Enjoyment is doing any activity where you are fully present and feel alive. You can find joy in any task, though most of us find it easier to enjoy certain tasks more than others.

Enthusiasm happens when you experience joy while working toward a goal or vision. Enthusiasm is a high-energy emotion that drives you when you are living your purpose.

It's important to note that enthusiasm is not the same as desiring the outcome. Enthusiasm is immersing yourself in your work without being attached to the result of your efforts. Tolle tells us that simply wanting the outcome creates stress. Enthusiasm means being present in the moment while moving toward a vision you believe in.

Action Steps

1. Review the extraordinary goal you set in chapter five. Ask yourself what feeling will create this result for you.

2. Think about what you need to believe in order to create this feeling. Write the thought in your journal.

3. Each day, review your new thought. Practice the thought and feeling.

Congratulations! You have completed the final action steps. Over the coming days, revisit this last exercise. You can also practice creating other beliefs that generate positive action energy. As you become more aware of your old patterns and practice new ones, you will learn how to create much bigger results in your business and finally achieve your full potential as an author.

15

CONCLUSION

In November of 2015, I published my first book. At the time, I did not know this would be the start of a new career as a writer and coach. In the four and half years since, I've published nine more books and learned everything I can about the writing and publishing world. Along the way I became fascinated with mindset and habits. I wanted to know why so many authors struggled despite their obvious potential.

Through my studies, interviews with other authors, coaching, and personal experience, I've uncovered two truths.

First, there's no one path to success. We're all unique and there are an infinite number of ways to create a profitable business as an author. But this is a good thing! It means you can build a writing career around your strengths and values. One that fits your life and your ambitions.

Second, there are three habits that all successful authors practice in some form. They are:

1. Act with purpose: Successful authors have a mission and take strategic action to fulfill their vision.

2. Create systems for success: Successful authors create systems so that essential tasks always get done.

3. Believe in yourself: Successful authors accept responsibility for their results and believe in their power to achieve the desired outcome, no matter what happens.

The third habit has been a game changer for me. By working on my inner state and practicing the three stages of self-belief, I've realized significant changes in my business and my personal life.

Now, it's your turn. This book describes the three habits and how to incorporate them into your writing life. Read each chapter, follow the action steps, and build your vision of success.

If you'd like more help, I've created some bonus resources for you. When you download the bonuses, you will get email access to me and an invitation to join my private community. I'd love to support you on your journey. It's my mission to help you do work you love. If that sounds like something you want, hop over to the bonus area at sallyannmiller.com/publish.

Go create your success as an author. There's no limit to the wealth and opportunities available to you. Your new life awaits.

ABOUT THE AUTHOR

Sally is a mom on a mission. She is passionate about answering the question, "Can modern moms have it all?" In a previous life, Sally worked for nineteen years as a project manager and business analyst in London and Silicon Valley. She has a Bachelor's Degree in Computer Science and a Master's Degree in Business Administration.

When her daughter was born, she discovered a new purpose. Sally left her corporate career to be a stay-at-home mom. She wanted to be a full-time mom to her kids. However, she missed the freedom and purpose that came from working. So Sally made a decision: she'd find a way to stay home with her kids and earn an income (without feeling torn between the two).

Sally is a self-confessed research geek and compulsive planner. She loves learning how stuff works, mastering new skills, and sharing her knowledge with others. Since leaving her nine-to-five, Sally has published ten bestselling books on Amazon (and counting).

You can find out more by visiting her website at sallyannmiller.com

Made in the USA
Las Vegas, NV
10 July 2022